WINNING THE JOB RACE

PATHWAYS THROUGH TRANSITION

JACK HEYDEN
SCOTT KANE

Gray Hair Management, LLC ®

ISBN   0-9766109-0-6

TABLE OF CONTENTS

INTRODUCTION

Need a job?

Want a better job?

Tired of the extra hours you have been working since your company had a 10% reduction in work force while the amount of work to be done has increased?

Do you feel like a "rookie" as you look for a job and need professional help finding the right opportunity?

Have you had no career growth and no advancement opportunities?

Have you reached the ceiling in your current position?

Are you underpaid, and are your talents and abilities underutilized and unrecognized?

Are you overdue for promotion or been passed over for promotion?

Have you been with one company for many years and don't recognize your options?

Are you concerned about your age?

Are you concerned about the future of your position and uncertain about your career choices in today's business climate?

Is your company going through organizational change, and you don't know where you stand?

If you answered yes to any of the twelve questions above, this book is for you. For the business professional ready to make a job or career change, <u>Winning the Job Race: Pathways Through Transition</u> provides a comprehensive program to help you successfully run the race for your next job opportunity.

In 2004, the Chicago Tribune reported, "the number of unemployed Americans remained stuck at 8 million, and almost 21% of them have been out of work for six months or more, the Labor Department said." Since 2001, the economy lost 2.6 million jobs while adding 1.7 million, a net loss of 900,000 jobs. There are two paths you can take with news like this: you can get frustrated and do nothing, or you can do something about it.

What is the message the American company is sending? When the share price is in trouble, cut staff. There is even further incentive to put people on the street with little notice. The top executives of the company typically receive even larger bonuses by producing better operating income, which was a direct result of terminating the employees they had previously "over hired."

If there are cheaper employees in India, China, or another third-world country to do your job, companies will find and hire them. Professional hockey players, baseball players, and basketball professionals will be the first to tell you about this type of global competition.

The question is not whether or not you accept the growing globalization and competitiveness of the work-force, but how you intend to confront such trends, survive their impact, and ultimately turn them into your own personal competitive advantage.

A professional athlete does not fear the competition. He or she gets up earlier, works out harder, and trains to win. The professional athlete is not at the mercy of "trends" in his or her sport. Imagine if athletes held a news conference to decry the increasing competitiveness in their sports. The world would laugh. Sports are supposed to be competitive, so what makes us think that business operates much differently? Because of this fact, we frequently use sports analogies when working with senior managers. You may not like sports, but business, like sports, is all about competition and winning.

At Gray Hair Management, LLC® (GHM) our business is helping business professionals win the job race. We provide coaching, mentoring and networking services. When senior managers are in transition or seeking a new opportunity, GHM helps them accelerate the process of identifying and securing their next job opportunity. When business professionals are working, GHM helps them build more successful, more satisfying and more profitable careers.

Each business professional needs to understand that he or she is their own primary organization to be concerned about. They are a walking repository of knowledge and achievement with objectives, goals and most importantly, accomplishments. Similar to a real organization, they need a personal career business plan that covers not just the next month or two, but plans for the rest of their professional career. In fact each person is an employee of his or her own company, the "My Personal Business" Company (MyPB).

In the following pages, you will be exposed to the GHM philosophy about how to successfully deal with the job realities facing 21st century business professionals. This book is based on our mentoring and coaching program, Pathways Through Transition^{sm}, which helps business professionals get a better job and build a more successful, satisfying career.

Statistically speaking, executives are apt to be "downsized" at least once every 1.8 to three years. For business professionals who have not attained the executive level yet, start planning to deal with this business fact now. Managers need to stop seeing the world in terms of "employees" and "employers." Recognize that you are merely renting your services to a particular institution for a particular period of time. Overnight you can become a "free agent" out of work with no guarantee of a job, period. In reality, and in most states, the only difference between a full time employee and a contract worker is who pays the benefits.

When you look at the employment world this way, a lot of preconceptions and misconceptions tend to fall away. You begin to understand that the "company" — whatever that is — does not owe you a living, nor is it at all sentimental about keeping you onboard simply for old times' sake.

Whether you have worked at your current position for a day, a year or a decade, there is always a potential event lurking in the wings that threatens your comfortable berth. A recession, a new product, a new business strategy, a merger, an acquisition, a wholesale management shuffle, your own high salary/benefits — any of these can unseat you at any time, and chances are one or more of these events will occur sooner or later.

Not so long ago, it was considered shameful to be out of work as a result of a company-initiated push. When someone used to lose his or her job, the first comment often heard was "You must have done something wrong," because for decades before no one was out of work unless they were flagrantly lacking in their position. These days, virtually no one cares if you're out of work because it is happening so often for reasons beyond your control. Virtually 99% of the people on the street today are there not because they did something wrong, but because the company decided to make a change.

If you know how to use today's unsettling employment trends to your advantage, then you can give yourself a leg up over others who have not taken the time and effort to think through how they are going to respond to a changing environment.

Why did we decide to write this book? We were senior executives who lost our jobs at the beginning of the 21st century. Although we began new careers, we met through networking , compared notes about what we had learned from our efforts to land jobs, and agreed that we should have gone about getting a job very differently than we had done.

Where did the name Gray Hair Management come from? While networking for a job in early 2000, (Scott's) youngest son introduced him to his 31-year old boss, a young and successful dot com entrepreneur working on his second million dollars. While sitting at lunch with the boss, Scott asked how a senior executive like himself, who was very technology savvy, could help dot coms or other emerging technology companies like his. After reflecting on the question, the young boss told Scott that there were a lot of young companies out there "who needed some gray hair." Scott had never heard that phrase used in that manner before, and the phrase struck a responsive cord. Soon he created a business card that read "Scott Kane, Gray Hair Manager for Young Companies."

Using this Gray Hair branding statement as his sales pitch when asked questions about his (My Personal Business) company, he began telling stories of his own career successes. He started having all kinds of people ask him about the kinds of work he had done, and whom he could recommend for projects that would help their own businesses. Because Scott was usually attending three to five networking events every week, he was meeting dozens of "gray hairs," and his database just kept growing. He also learned that 1) young companies did indeed have a lot of growing pains where some gray hair help was desperately needed, and 2) those young companies often had no money.

When you finish reading this book, we both hope we have helped you get a great job (if you are looking), as well as take better control of your personal business career. Everyone wants to be a pro at his/her chosen profession. We can help you achieve that goal.

Jack Heyden, Scott Kane
Gray Hair Management LLC

CHAPTER 1
PREPARING TO RUN THE RACE

WINNING THE MIND GAME

Right from the beginning, it's important that business professionals change the way they think about their situation. They are not, in fact, recently terminated or "fired" or in need of a job change, but they are instead taking the opportunity to be reinvented as business athletes with enormous experience and competency in their field(s). Unlike those people we usually think of as athletes, true business athletes are those who can reposition their emotional reactions to their professional setbacks quickly, and succeed in finding their next job opportunity more quickly.

Over the past several years, the 21st century company has learned that no one really cares if they treat their employees badly other than the affected employees. In fact, when a company reduces its workforce by 1,000 employees, who is there to take them to task? No one! In fact, instead of being penalized, they actually reap a benefit. Their stock price goes up. When the airline industry laid off more than 100,000 employees post-911, our government gave them a $5 billion bailout package. Why would a company not take unfair advantage of its workforce when there is little or no downside risk to dumping them on the street?

As a result, every business professional has to recognize that the "relationship contract" between today's 21st century company and each employee has been altered for the foreseeable future. A relationship contract consists of the mutual expectations established between either an individual and another individual, an individual and a group, or a group and another group in order to try and clarify their relationship.

A relationship contract formed between two parties essentially breaks down into a list of four questions to be answered:

1. *What do I expect to get from you in the relationship?*

2. *What do I expect to give to you in the relationship?*

3. *What do you expect to get from me in the relationship?*

4. *What do you expect to give to me in the relationship?*

It's easy to know what we personally expect to give and get from the relationship. Learning the other's give and get may not always be so easy, and this can cause the relationship contract to break down or even end. The breakdown in the relationship contract can either be a result of a personnel change, an organizational change, or a financial change.

Consider what happens to the terminated professional. For many, they are out of work for the very first time — with or without some kind of termination package to partially ease the shock. They've gone from being successful business professionals to job-hunting rookies.

Quite often they never saw it coming. The individual was a critical part of the organization that just let them go. They were working their proverbial tail off for the company's benefit. In many cases, they may well have had an idea that something bad was going to happen. Yet, when you have invested perhaps 15-30 years in a company, your skill set and your mindset are focused around your job, and denial tends to take precedence over the reality that your position is about to end.

So what can you do about it?

For starters:

1 Get over it, and get moving. One of the most frustrating things we see in our business is the senior manager who, given a twelve-month severance package, decides to first take a three-month vacation. Too often this turns out to be a poor decision, if for no other reason than most executives lose the opportunity to work with executive search companies, most of who do not work with unemployed executives who have been out of work more than 60 to 90 days.

It is not easy to get past the emotional issues and move on. A certain percentage of professionals lack the personal makeup to quickly "mourn and move on." When a positive amount of abasement (the ability to self criticize) gets too high and it leads to self doubt, we know that extra work (and probably time) will be required to move that individual along the career path. One of our coaching clients took almost six months to fully acknowledge that his layoff was not his fault. Consequently, his personal transition program took that much longer to complete.

2 Dedicate yourself to getting in shape in order to run what literally becomes a very competitive race to get a new job.

3 Know your personal business strengths and weaknesses completely in addition to knowing the professional job currency value you bring to the table for a new employer.

4 Keep an eye on what is happening to your morale as you work through this transition process. There is a Morale Curve, and it is important to recognize its potential impact on your situation. The Morale Curve was first identified by Dr. Karl Menninger when he was doing research on problems happening to the original Americans recruited into the Peace Corps. People often joined the Peace Corps with high,

unrealistically positive expectations about changing the world. When reality set in, usually four to six months after joining and being out in the field alone, morale dropped quickly. Although most people learned to cope and shovel out of his/her low morale situation, others got sick or did more drastic things when they could not cope with their own situation.

How can we use knowledge of the Morale Curve to deal with job loss? When going through a job transition, it is important to avoid getting too emotionally high at the beginning of the transition process as you prepare for getting a new career opportunity. Too often, the individual may set unrealistic goals concerning length of time required to get the next job. Also, it is important to recognize that once you get well into the actual transition process, it is pretty easy to hit the wall one or more times during the journey. You need to know how to deal with those low morale situations also.

5 Plan your own Pathway Through Transition as though you are positioning yourself to win a marathon competition. Think of this analogy. When a major marathon such as those held in Chicago, New York and Boston occurs, which of the runners is placed in the front of the race? Of course, they place the probable winners up front. The front rows are reserved for those who have been ranked before, have won before, and the ones with the most experience. If these runners are so good, perhaps they should be placed at the back of the race to make a real race of it. They are not placed in the back of the race because there is little chance that they will be able to get through the throngs of less proficient runners in front of them, let alone win the race. Positioning yourself to get a job requires the same strategy in that you have to be considered by the sponsor of the race, the new employer, as one of the potential winners going in so that you are placed in the front of the race when the race starts. If you're not, then you go to the middle or the back of the pack, and the chances of winning diminish greatly.

THE MYTH OF EXECUTIVE LEADERSHIP

You are in charge of your career, no one else - not your boss, not your company's CEO, just you. Trust anyone else, and you may suffer the consequences.

John Chambers, CEO of Cisco Systems may have been The Wonder Boy of all business wonder boys as we entered the new millennium. Cisco was an investor's best fantasy, racking up unbelievable share price increases quarter after quarter. Yet, with Mr. Chambers at the helm, Cisco Systems then experienced a major league stock price meltdown that saw its price plummeting about 80 percent in a span of 12 months ending March, 2001. Chambers went from being quoted on CNN seemingly every week to becoming the new starring character in the business edition of, "Where in the World is Carmen San Diego." So what happened?

Jack Welch, now retired CEO of General Electric is another example. How big was Jack? Jack was so big that if there were a Business Executive Leadership Hall of Fame, the Nominating Committee would have waived the five-year rule after executives retire before they can be admitted. With Jack still at the helm, GE experienced its own sizable stock price meltdown that saw the price shrink about 30 percent in a span of six months ending March, 2001. That was before news of the extra perks Welch was getting while at the helm were disclosed.

So what happened? These CEOs (and others such as Carly Fiorina of Hewlett Packard, which had its own 60 percent stock price meltdown in a twelve-month period) did not take a stupid pill overnight. They are very talented executives. What happened in large part was that they were around long enough to fall victim to another of the many

80/20 rules (let's call it "The Business Pond Rule") in business life. That 80/20 rule was nicely summed up by Sydney Schoeffler, then Managing Director, The Strategic Planning Institute, when he wrote that, "The laws of the marketplace determine 80% of the variance in operating results across different businesses . . . This means the served characteristics of the served marketplace, of the business itself, and of its competitors, constitute about 80% of the reasons for success or failure [i.e., being in the right business pond], and the operating skill or luck of the management constitutes about 20%."

It is for this reason (among others) that employees are often unprepared for the impact of poor earnings downturns and company layoffs. We're not advocating that you live in fear of job loss, only that you regard your professional life with hard-headed realism. Wishful thinking is not going to prevent the axe from cutting your position or put food on the table when your resources are drained. You have to take control of your career.

Your job skills should always be up-to-date, as should your resume and computer skills. You should always be cultivating your personal and professional network — constantly building a database using a contact manager software program in order to organize and accommodate the different corporate professionals you have met — and following through with those whom you want to meet again and again and again.

You need to take control of both your current job situation (if you have one) and your career right now. This is like you becoming Jimmy Chitwood, the quiet hero of the movie, "Hoosiers."

The small town high school basketball team from Hickory, Indiana is playing against the top-ranked team from one of Indiana's largest cities for the state championship. There's less than 30 seconds left in the state championship game. It is going to take a clutch basket for the miracle of the century to occur. The Hickory coach,

Norman Dale, played by Gene Hackman, has called the play during a timeout, and no one moves. All the ball players know the play is not going to work. They realize the only way to have a chance to win the game is to get the ball into Jimmy Chitwood's hands, the star of the team, and stay out of his way while he does his thing.

Jimmy, who has carried the team into the playoffs, agrees that he needs to take the last shot. The coach considers the situation, and changes the play. Jimmy lets the play clock tick down inside 10 seconds, makes his move, shoots, wins the game. Pandemonium!

Why connect the movie Hoosiers with today's business professionals? Hoosiers ultimately comes down to finding out who on the team wanted the ball when the season and the game were on the line. Great athletes live for the day when everything rests on their shoulders, while good athletes are just happy to play second fiddle as the pressure mounts. Become the Jimmy Chitwood of your MyPB.

We often compare the race for your next job to a sports competition. The big difference between the job search and a sports competition is there is no medal for second place in job search.

TAKING CONTROL

Let's focus on three primary ways to take more control over your career success:

1 Start your own career personal business.

2 Create your personal career business plan.

3 Create your personal business organization chart.

Why do you need to think about starting your own personal business? One of the things business professionals who are out of work fail to realize is that they are never unemployed. Looking for a job is a full time occupation, albeit one you're not being paid for (unless you have severance). Let's understand why.

Even when professionals are unemployed, they always remain an owner of their own personal company, MyPB. The problem for many professionals is either they don't really know that they are the sole proprietor of this company, or they have not been running MyPB like an honest-to-goodness business.

Many of us grew up with the premise that if you went to work for a company, and you did a good job, then you could stay there as long as you'd want. Instead, executives are realizing the company sending them a W-2 at the end of the year is not going to be their lifetime employer. They also learn that their careers will not magically fall into place by divine intervention, luck or with the guidance of their W-2 bosses.

White-collar professionals must realize the game has changed. If you don't get that ball into your own hands, your game and the season can be over as early as the next day. In reality, the next person to fire you needs to be you.

Once you have decided it's a good idea to start your MyPB Company, you need to concentrate on the mission of your business, and that's getting you a job, or a better job. One might think that since the MyPB company is all yours, your position in the company is that of CEO/President/Owner. This is not quite correct. In fact, your real job position in the MyPB Company is Vice President of Sales and Marketing. And, the product you are selling is YOU.

Like any good company, you need a personal mission statement that the people you meet can immediately understand when you explain it to them within 30 seconds or less. This is your Elevator Speech.

A throwback to the turn of the 20th century, the Elevator Speech was the sales pitch the suitcase-carrying salesman used when he met you in an elevator on the 10th floor, and was able to sell you his wares by the time you reached the lobby. In your own MyPB situation, you have to know and be able to speak to your product, you, in a very short and meaningful time. With the average listener's attention span of 30 seconds, you must "sell" your wares within the 30 second period.

As it relates to career mentoring and coaching, it quickly became clear to us that:

1 Although professionals understand and enthus-iastically support the need for traditional businesses to have a strategic business plan, virtually no one has written one for their own MyPB business. As professionals move up the ranks and become senior-level executives, they often authorize the expenditure of many thousands of dollars to retain outside consultants and/or hire full-time employees to develop strategic business plans. They also spend many hours of their own time thinking about, developing and presenting business plans to senior management and board members in order to promote their own careers and maximize shareholder value. And yet, business professionals virtually spend no time thinking through and writing down their own MyPB strategic business plan.

2 When senior managers do think about their business career, they often fall victim to the "Next Job Syndrome." Just about every person thinks about his or her career in a working forward manner, rather than a working backwards process. In other words, the business professional mostly thinks in terms of what his/her next job is going to be. This is very under-standable, especially if you're out of work. There is unbelievable pressure on you to put food on the table when you're out of work, so the Next Job Syndrome is a natural outcome. For anyone currently working, the Next Job Syndrome is still typically the way we think. That's because most experienced managers who change jobs while currently working often hear about that new job from an executive search recruiter, not because they decided to take charge of their own career by developing and then following their personal business plan.

Instead, the forward-thinking business professional should be identifying the last job necessary to reach his/her end-of-career goal. Once you identify your target last career job, you can now address the question of how you're going to get there by working backwards. As you do so, keep in mind that the average "life" of a current executive job is 1.8 to three years.

For example, Jamie Logan wants to work 13 more years and retire as a CFO for a mid-sized company. Working backwards, Jamie's job prior to CFO might be corporate controller and, prior to that, division controller. Currently Jamie is a division finance manager. Jamie's Pathways Throught Transition job chart appears at the end of this chapter.

3 Generally, only two percent of senior managers we have met with since starting GHM have a very reasonable idea of where they are going to end up in terms of their last career job, and usually they do not have it written down. So if you're serious about your MyPB business plan, including your ultimate career goals, get it down on paper.

You are also putting your personal business plan in written form in order to get the ball into your own hands and take control of your career. What's next? There is a need for executives to decide whom they need on their personal MyPB organizational chart in order to win the race for the next job and for maximum career success.

In business, maximum success also may not happen without the best coach available to help the business athlete. Recognizing that being in the right pond can be eighty percent of the formula for business success, it still means that great management is essential to achieving maximum business success. Senior business executives can look to their board of directors, advisory boards, management consultants, and executive mentors and coaches to add the extra twenty percent needed to win.

Business professionals also have to determine the role of coaching in their own MyPB businesses. Most senior managers, consciously or unconsciously, have decided they will achieve their career goals by being their own coach. This is despite the fact that most successful business executives have usually sought help from a variety of expert sources, especially when the company was paying for it.

Using a sports analogy, there has never been a modern day professional sports winner, a champion, without a coach standing close by. The ice skater, Michelle Kwan tried once to go it alone and not use the services of a coach, and it didn't work. She performed well, but she did not win.

It is also interesting to note that individuals use coaches for all kinds of important events in their personal lives, events such as: big dollar vacations (travel agents); weddings (party planners); financial security (personal financial planners, financial advisers, lawyers, life insurance agents); surgery (doctors and hospital teams); losing weight (Weight Watchers, personal trainers, Jenny Craig). Yet, most professionals avoid using business coaches when it comes to their livelihood.

Decide if you need a coach or several coaches on your organization chart as part of your advisory team. Also determine who should be the Chairman of the Board. We often recommend that this should be your spouse if you are married because your job in the MyPB company is primarily sales and marketing; and you will have your hands full with those responsibilities.

The bottom line is that each professional looking for a new opportunity needs to:

◆ Try to work for a company in the right pond.

◆ Be ready to move on if you feel your pond is turning into a swamp.

- ◆ Create your own MyPB organization (see below).
- ◆ Avoid the Next Job Syndrome, and work backwards to achieve your career goals.
- ◆ Put your personal business plan in writing.
- ◆ Decide if and when you need a business coach or mentor.
- ◆ Think carefully about who is going to be on your personal advisory board of directors, then create that board.

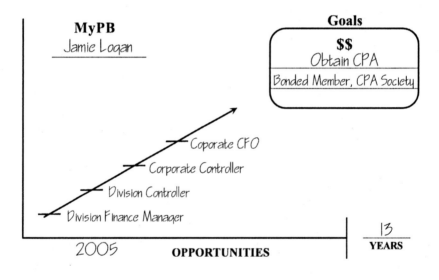

CHAPTER 2
GETTING FOCUSED

In order to seek out that next job opportunity and implement a more successful career plan, you need to truly understand yourself, how you relate to others, what unique skill sets you offer to an employer, and what you need to improve upon for a chance at even greater success. This self analysis is akin to a business doing a SWOT (strengths, weaknesses, opportunities, threats) Analysis during a business strategic planning process.

Business professionals need to understand how they fit into the world of business, and what they need to do to cultivate success. The degree to which you can successfully accomplish this initial task will go a long way toward determining how well you manage your own Pathway Through Transition and beyond.

That is why Phase One of the GHM Pathways Through Transition Program is titled "Getting Focused."

Here is an initial checklist of items you should ask yourself (and write down answers to) as you develop your own Pathways Through Transition Program:

◆ Your business strengths.

◆ Your business areas to improve.

◆ The influence organizations (especially your last organization) have had on your past (and future) business behaviors.

◆ The ideal organizational culture/climate you are seeking in your next job.

◆ The quantifiable contributions (measurable impact primarily on revenues, expenses and quality) you have made to each of the companies you worked for in the past. (*Our coaching clients will be the first to tell you that this step is often the hardest step they complete as they go through the Pathways program.*)

As much as you might want to write a resume quickly and get going on that next job journey, each individual needs to first take an objective, detailed look back at his or her past to sort out positive and negative behaviors, to emphasize strengths and leverage weaknesses, and to measure one's accomplishments in order to define your total job currency value to a company.

As a business professional begins the journey forward to seeking the next great job opportunity, that is the time to remember why people get hired in the first place. In today's business climate, the only reason you are going to be offered a position is because someone perceives you are the solution to their problem. No one today is hired unless he fulfils a need and solves a problem. In order to become the best solution to someone's business problem, one has to be able to formulate a better value proposition than anyone else competing for that job. In order to do that, you need the best answers to those typical questions asked by inter-viewers. Some of these questions are:

1. *If I met someone who knew you very well professionally, how would they describe you to me?*

2. *How would you describe your number one personal competitive advantage over other job candidates?*

3. *What is one of your most significant work-related accomplishments?*

4. *What is one of the more difficult problems you had to solve in a past assignment?*

5. *What is one of your personal areas of improvement that you're working on?*

6. Where do you see yourself professionally in three years?

7. Since I have hundreds of job candidates to choose from, why should I choose you?

8. Would you agree that you are overqualified and too expensive for this job assignment?

In order to answer those questions you better know yourself inside and out, where you have been in your career and what kind of quantifiable value you brought to each company you've worked for. For today's Gray Hair gladiator out on the battlefield in search of a job, that begins with initially measuring your strengths and weaknesses. There are many assessment models used by businesses. We accomplish this for clients by doing a psychological assessment, the Need-Press Analysis Profile©, developed by Dr. Morris Aderman, that has the unique ability to not only measure executive business attributes, but also measure the executive's ability to evaluate how organizations function as well as defining what they perceive to be the attributes of high-performance organizations.

Each senior manager is individually benchmarked against a database of 1,800 "successful" (VP or higher, two significant promotions in the last five years) executives. 18 factors are evaluated from both an individual and from an organizational perspective. Those 18 factors are:

1 Abasement: level of self criticism.

2 Achievement: level at which goals and standards should be set.

3 Affiliation: degree to which employees socialize and build relationships.

4 Aggression: using belittlement/verbal abuse to get things done.

5 Autonomy: freedom to be unconventional, innovative.

6 Change: to do new and different things.

7 Counteraction: overcoming obstacles by mobilizing resources available.

8 Defensiveness: to defend oneself against blame or belittlement.

9 Deference: to admire and willingly follow a leader or business expert.

10 Dominance: to lead, influence and direct others.

11 Endurance: to follow through and complete a task or problem.

12 Exhibition: to attract attention, to vie for visibility (the degree to which "it's all about me).

13 Caution: fear of failure, to delay decisions.

14 Analytical: to analyze motives and feelings (one's own and others).

15 Helpfulness: to reach out and assist others.

16 Order: to plan and arrange goals and tasks appropriately.

17 Rejection: to reserve the right to exclude others, to be reluctant to express one's own opinions.

18 Dependency: to expect others to help you when situations arise.

Each factor is measured on a scale ranging from zero (lowest) to nine (highest) so that executives find out how they "stack up" against 1,800 other executives. There is a "range" of scores identified for each of the 18 business factors representing where about 70 percent of the executives in the database fell. This enables each individual to be "benchmarked" against the database to evaluate how they perform compared to other business executives.

Based on the results, executives understand their professional strengths and weaknesses. They understand the influence their most recent (or current) organization has on their performance (either positive or negative). Executives also develop a comprehensive description of the "ideal" organization that will enable them to attain peak performance.

Here's an example of how the assessment results works. Terry is a proven, talented, knowledgeable, highly compensated executive working for a number of years for a well known company that was forced to go through a reduction in force. Terry was confident, yet sufficiently self critical (Abasement), a high goal setter (Achievement), somewhat of a loner (Affiliation), totally non hostile (Aggression), innovative/creative [yet unwilling to delegate the same level of innovation to subordinates] (Autonomy), resistant to changing conditions (Change), strongly committed to win and overcome obstacles (Counteraction), non defensive (Defensiveness), respectful of authority figures (Deference), comfortable in a leadership role [but not wanting anyone to exert leadership from above over him] (Dominance), strongly committed to following through and completing tasks (Endurance), low profile (Exhibition), able to take appropriate levels of risk (Caution), reasonably interested in understanding the feelings of others (Analytical), not at all interested in extending a helping hand to others [even though intellectually knows better] (Helpfulness), well organized, a good planner (Order), very aloof [yet knows should not be so aloof] (Rejection], and comfortable seeking out appropriate levels of help and support from others (Dependency).

Terry has many excellent executive strengths. Terry does have two potentially critical flaws. First, Terry was going to continue to have problems with certain managers because of the "comfortable in a leadership role, but not wanting anyone to exert leadership from above" tendency. In other words, "I like being in charge, but don't try being in charge of me and looking over my shoulder if you are my boss." Most leaders are also "comfortable in a leadership role" themselves, so they have certain expect-ations in terms of an employee's willingness to be led. Since good hiring managers are trained to look for specific leadership characteristics, Terry could have some inter-viewing problems during Terry's own transition.

Second, Terry's personal balance between helping others (Helpfulness) and asking for help in return (Dependency) was the exact opposite of the overwhelming majority of leaders in business. Leaders typically prefer to give (Helpfulness) a little bit more than they get back from others (Dependency), so that at the end of the year everyone else ends up with a slight IOU in their "relationship account" with the leader. When the reverse is true, everyone tends to see the other person as more of a "taker" rather than as a "giver." People react negatively to takers. Since getting a job is all about being willing to follow the pay-it-forward rule (We say one has to give fives times greater than they take, but the one take will be five times greater than they gave.), Terry will have a bigger challenge becoming an effective networker.

Can a manager or executive successfully work around these development weaknesses? Sure, but in order to do so, one first needs to know what those weaknesses are. Knowledge is power, and with that knowledge, one can learn to leverage his/her strengths and compensate for his/her weaknesses. (The business professional can also learn how to use this information to more effectively interview for a job.)

We also recommend that business professionals go back and evaluate how successful they have been in their business careers. We suggest this be done by having you go through an RSA (Results, Situation, Action) exercise... one of those exercises that is easy for everyone to understand, but sometimes very difficult to implement. This type of assessment process is not new. It has been around for years. Based on the thousands of resumes we have seen, the greater majority of those resume writers fail to apply the RSA approach in detailing the successful history of one's career. Many professionals have difficulty adding quantitative metrics to their own accomplishments, an absolute necessity in knowing the value you bring to the table.

Try it yourself. Think of a situation where you were required to complete a series of actions in a certain way using your business knowledge and skills in order to accomplish a meaningful result. The trick here is to be able to describe a result in such a way that you end up with a significant, quantitative end result (or metric) that measures what you accomplished in terms of revenue, expense or quality impact benefiting the employer. That is the R in RSA. The R's also become the bullet points in your resume. Then describe in writing the situation (challenge, opportunity, problem) you were faced with in only one short sentence. That is the S in RSA. The key is to be able to create an immediate connection between the R and the S so that later, during a job interview, you can quickly help the job interviewer understand the connection between the S (which the interviewer has not seen because it is not on your resume) and the R (which is on the resume in bullet point form). Then use some space to write out the actions you took (and also describe the skills and knowledge you utilized) that led to the result you/your team achieved. That is the A in RSA.

Executives find out it is not that easy to complete this exercise of summarizing one's measurable acts in a career going back 15 or 20 years. In fact, if we were aware of this RSA process when we were rising through the corporate ranks, we would have kept a little folder in our desks where we would place post-it notes or 3x5 cards every time we had accomplished something of value for the company. Today, that folder would be overflowing with little reminders about how good we really are, and writing a resume today would be a whole lot easier.

The bottom line to remember is that you need to:

1 Start working on answers to the tough questions you anticipate hiring managers, headhunters (search firms), and people you will network with might ask you as soon as possible.

2 Understand and write out your personal SWOT Analysis, which should include your strengths, professional areas to develop, the impact organizations had (and will have) on your performance, and the kind of "ideal" organization you want to work for.

3 Write out RSAs recapping your accomplishments. Most resumes we work on with our clients require about 16 completed RSAs in order to create a very powerful resume. Start this process immediately. The longer you wait, the harder it will be to remember or obtain the metrics that quantify the accomplishment.

CHAPTER 3

PACKAGING YOURSELF FOR JOB SUCCESS: PERSONAL INTEGRATED MARKETING

In our dealings with executives in transition, we mentioned earlier that the only reason people get hired is because a hiring manager sees the individual as the solution to one or more of the company's business problems. There are a lot of other professionals who will be competing against you for that job also thinking they are the best solution to the problem. So, you will need to be different than them. Think of a way to create your own unique PCA (personal competitive advantage). Differentiate yourself from everyone else in such a way that you become both unique and very desirable to the right people.

To achieve this, you need to create an integrated marketing program for your job search. You can create your MyPB company, define your mission, build an organization team to support you, know your strengths and weaknesses, measure your past successes by doing RSAs, and still struggle with your job and career search if you can't differentiate yourself from your competition sufficiently to become the best solution to someone's problem.

PERSONAL BRANDING

We call this the GHM "Can of Soup" approach. As you compete for a job, think of yourself as a can of soup, perched on the shelf of a supermarket. There you are, on the shelf with hundreds of other cans of soup. What goes through the mind of the consumer to select that one can of soup and place it into the shopping cart (the cart represents the job interview)? In marketing, it's called the differentiators of the product. Generally, consumer products have many differentiators enticing consumers to take them off the shelf. Remember, getting into the cart only represents the interview. You still need to get to the check-out counter and get the job. Those who fail at the interview usually wind up being placed back on the shelf.

The mission of personal branding is to identify those differences about you that few others in your area of expertise can match. Be different, and make sure you promote those differentiators so that the buyer (the hiring manager) will select you over the competition. This is a true sales and marketing effort for the product, you.

It does not matter what your true expertise is. It can be information technology, operations, human resources, strategic planning or supply chain management. You can be great at what you do. If you cannot brand yourself sufficiently to create a powerful PCA and then develop a comprehensive packaging program to get yourself into that shopping cart, you'll reduce your chances of getting to the next phase of the journey, which is going through the checkout counter (getting a job offer). And this is where so many people fall short in their efforts to get a job: sales and marketing.

Ironically, many of the business professionals we meet who seem to have the greatest problem creating a personal brand identity and personal marketing campaign are marketing professionals. Ironically, they spend their business career marketing products and services of companies, yet they have trouble practicing this craft for themselves. So what is a brand? In an excellent book, Selling the Invisible, author Harry Beckwith wrote that "a brand is more than a symbol. In the public's eye, a brand is a warranty. It is a promise that the service carrying that brand will live up to its name, and perform . . . A service is a promise, and building a brand builds your promise." So figure out your personal brand, and make it memorable.

The key question to answer in order to begin creating your personal branding is "So what do you really do?" By answering that question, you are on your way to creating the key marketing documents you will need to market yourself: resume, handbill, cover letters, business cards.

We have a lot of fun working with clients to create a distinctive, personal brand along with a tag line clarifying the brand that is accurate and comfortable for the executive to use in networking and job search situations. Here's a few we especially like:

Safecracker: Unlocking the wealth between customers and products through marketing.

Improvenator: Taking under performing companies to the next level.

Executive Helmsman: Steering businesses to the next higher level.

Corporate Reputarian: Helping corporations and non profits build strong reputations and stakeholder value.

Wings, Wheels and Rudders: Improving revenue, profit and performance for cruise, travel, cargo and aviator companies.

In each of the cases above, these executives have created a memorable brand with a tag line, and each had the credentials to deliver on the brand promise summarized in the follow-up tagline. Earlier we wrote about the need for a personal elevator speech (the sales pitch the early 20th century suitcase-carrying salesman used when he met someone in the elevator). You are now ready to integrate your personal brand and tag line into your elevator speech.

If you are having trouble telling someone you meet for the first time in an elevator, "Hi, my name is Ralph, and I am a safecracker," you can always blame someone else for your brand. In this case you can instead say, "Hi, my name is Ralph. I help companies unlock the wealth between customers and products through marketing. In fact, some people who know me well characterize me as a safecracker."

Bottom line: make it work so that you are comfortable saying it and believing it.

RESUMES

Resumes seem so easy. The purpose of your resume is to get a face-to-face meeting with someone seeking a solution to a business problem. So you choose a standard format and write up an Executive Summary, create a Work Experience and Selected Accomplishments section followed by an Education section. You may sneak in Certifications and/or Technical Skills sections as well depending upon your experience and job expertise. Make it two pages or less. Simple. So why do most resumes fail to get that interview for the executive? Most resumes fail to get noticed by the reader because either:

1 The Executive Summary gives the reader no clue what the person really does.

2 The Executive Summary takes longer than six to ten seconds to read and/or puts the reader to sleep without creating a PCA.

3 Accomplishments are written as features (which describe the situation and actions of your success story) rather than benefits (the results delivered).

4 Work Experience is formatted in such a way that the reader a) gets confused about what you did and/or b) is unimpressed with your job responsibilities.

5 The Work Experience section leaves out earlier professional positions in an attempt to conceal the candidate's true age or to avoid short, unsuccessful work assignments.

6 Work Experience dates are omitted as a tactic in order to conceal the candidate's age. (We once met a talented young professional, age 33, and this individual listed no years in the resume experience section because of advice received from an "expert" in resume writing to always hide one's true age.)

7 The Education section leaves out college/graduate school graduation dates (often as another tactic to hide your age).

8 You are one of 700-2,000 people responding to an internet ad being screened by a human resources staff member with two years business experience who, through no fault of her/his own, has no clear understanding of what the real job requires in terms of experience, knowledge, skills and behaviors.

The reality is that at some point in time the hiring manager (sooner than you think if the person is a real veteran) will assess your accomplishments, and then reject you if you are not suited for the job. Remember, it doesn't matter if you think you're a perfect fit, when in reality, they have to believe you're perfect for the position. In fact, if you have gaps in your resume, you may be rejected immediately because the evaluator assumes you are hiding additional factors which may be more significant than age. If someone else has more measurable accomplishments, your chances for an interview drop. If you make the screener or hiring manager work too hard to figure out what you do and/or your PCA, your chances for an interview drop.

So how do you improve a resume? For starters, we suggest that you:

1 Create your PCA prior to finalizing your resume so that you know what you want to build your Executive Summary around.

2 Keep the Executive Summary short and to the point (the reader may only give you less than 10 seconds of total time to read the entire resume the first time, so select your words carefully).

3 Use the results section from your RSAs (that you should have written out prior to doing the resume) to become the bullet points you select as your accomplishments (remember: the resume is your "highlight reel" and not the entire "game tape" of your business career).

4 Learn how to use the margins and other features of your word processing software to format your resume (or find someone who knows how), so that it is easy to look at and quickly understand.

5 List all of your work experience and years worked at each professional job (again… good resume readers figure out your age anyway, and this helps avoid the risk of the reader assuming you have more than your age that you're trying to hide).

6 Show your education dates (unless you really are trying to hide something which will most likely be discovered later on anyway by any good interviewer).

To give you an example of the different impact you can create in the mind of the resume reader, here are some actual bullet point accomplishments we revised to have a stronger impact:

BEFORE	REVISED
"Due to leadership void, took leadership role and not only created strategic plans, but also directed all financial, information technology human resources, and operational areas. Efforts resulted in successful contract negotiation with client for the "Values Supporting Our Brands" project."	"Converted a $50,000 consulting engagement into a $1 million year-long strategic branding initiative by working with the client to develop an outcome driven project architecture."

BEFORE	REVISED
"Initiated strategic recommendation and creative development that led to first locally developed pan-regional campaign for Intel."	"Successfully developed Intel's first locally produced pan-regional campaign, which contributed to agency winning worldwide account. Campaign introduced new Pentium Processor, generating sales for upgrades."
"New business wins included Visa and Kraft/General Foods."	"Increased Hong Kong agency annual billings by over $5.2 million by leading new business team which won Citibank Visa and Kraft/General Foods pan-Asia accounts."
"Negotiated a payment of $30 million in stock that would be registered at issuance in exchange for an intellectual property license plus an additional $30 million in stock and royalties for assistance in developing the company's next generation product. Follow-on software implementation are expected to generate over $600 million in services revenue through 2006."	"Booked $30 million in revenue at the closing of a strategic alliance deal projected to generate an additional $600 million in revenue."

As an analogy, think of the resume in the same light as the TV sportscaster in the nightly newscast. The sportscaster has two minutes out of a total of thirty to deliver the sports. Is he going to tell you about the walks or the home runs? The resume should be used to tell the prospective employer about your home runs. Your mission here is to arouse enough attention that they will want to talk with you and find out about the rest of your career.

HANDBILLS

A handbill is a sales sheet about you. It is most effectively used when you are working on the assumption there is no available job position. Similar to a catalog sheet, it briefly details the benefits you bring to the table. Since your resume is focused on your past accomplishments (and designed to be used when there is a job position available), the handbill instead focuses on the future. Think of the resume as the "features" statement, while the handbill is the "benefits" statement. All good sales people will tell you that you cannot sell a product without detailing the features and the benefits. By adding a simple list of targeted companies, the handbill is also the standard handout at job transition networking events.

A handbill should provide answers to three essential questions:

Who am I?

What am I seeking?

How can I add value to a company?

Answers to these three questions form the three sections of your handbill. The "Who am I?" answer can be gleaned from the Executive Summary section of your resume. The "What am I seeking?" answer needs to help the reader understand the challenges and opportunities you are seeking in your next job assignment. The "How can I add value to a company?" section is a chance for you to select the most appropriate features and benefits that will catch the reader's eye.

Here's an example of a handbill:

Jamie Logan

1234 N Elm Street ♦ Anywhere, IL 12345
612/555-1234
jamiel@isp.com

SENIOR EXECUTIVE FOR WINGS, WHEELS AND RUDDERS

WHO I AM . . .

A versatile senior executive with strong revenue, profit and performance improvement experience in cruise, travel, cargo and aviation organizations. Proven record of leadership, turnaround, new product development, cost reduction, customer care and quality improvement. Effective leader of international, multi-cultural teams.

WHAT I AM LOOKING FOR . . .

A senior executive position in a small to mid-sized service-sector company seeking to improve profitability, quality and customer service.

The primary challenges of the opportunity should include:

♦ A company-wide commitment to service excellence and market leadership — **Quality and Customer Focus.**

♦ Profitable expansion into new markets and opportunities — **Company Growth.**

- Aligning each tier of the organization with the company's vision, mission and corporate objectives — **Company Direction.**

- Finding unique and creative solutions to real-world challenges in pursuit of company goals — **Structural and Logistical Challenges.**

- The opportunity to lead and motivate through direct personal contact with all team members — **Hands-on Leadership.**

- The opportunity for **Professional Growth.**

HOW I CAN ADD VALUE . . .

- Using my P&L experience to quickly **increase revenues, reduce costs and maximize ROI.**

- Turning my market expertise into development and introduction of successful **new products and services.**

- Using my leadership skills to direct and **motivate sales & marketing teams** to optimize revenues.

- Leveraging my people skills for improved customer retention through regular key account contact.

- Applying my **strategic expansion** experience through corporate acquisition and integration.

- Focusing my operational experience on **strengthening management controls** through improved reporting systems.

When do you use a handbill? A great time is either when you are at a group networking session, prior to a one-on-one networking meeting you have set up, as a leave behind for that networking meeting, or as the lead page on your personal website (something we recommend everyone obtain). The handbill is a perfect substitute for the resume if you are involved in a networking meeting instead of a job interview.

Seems simple enough. Unfortunately, we meet lots of senior managers who end up getting "helpful hints" from other job seekers or job experts suggesting they add a few tidbits to the handbill. Suggestions often include:

1 "Add a short list of your accomplishments."

2 "It would be helpful to provide the reader with a brief job history segment."

3 "Since you have great education credentials [often from 20 or 30 years ago], you should include those credentials."

4 "Put down 15-20 target companies to help the reader understand who you want to work for." (We are okay with a short list of targeted companies added to your handbill for a structured job transition networking meeting, but it can hurt you on a one-on-one with a working executive. We suggest that you actually develop two, not one, handbills to prepare you for one-on-one meetings as well as for structured job transition meetings.)

All of a sudden, you end up with a semi-condensed version of your resume combined with some extra things thrown in rather than a handbill that can be dynamic and set you apart from the next person.

COVER LETTERS

We offer one critical observation about successful cover letters: successful cover letters are written from the reader's point of view. Great salespeople know this and live by it. Remember, one of your MyPB job position hats is VP Sales. Also remember:

◆ You will have the urge to wax eloquent in order to dazzle your reader with your fantastic knack for prose and to present your great skills. Don't. It will not help. As one of our favorite senior executive search executives recently told us, "Make the letter short because I am going to look at the attached resume for the answers to my questions rather than your cover letter (we know, lots of disagreement here on the importance of "killer" cover letters) anyway."

◆ You will have the urge to tell the reader your whole story. Don't. Save the features for the interview so that you have a reason to meet. If you tell your whole story, why should there be a meeting?

◆ You will have the urge to somehow convince the reader you should meet even though you only possess eight of the ten job requirements listed for the job (which will actually turn out to be twelve requirements, those we call the "Hidden Bunny"). The reader could be getting anywhere from perhaps 200 to 2,000 other cover letters with a resume attached, and the reader probably specified that you must have all eleven job requirements. All you will doing is clog up the resume "pipeline" and make it even more difficult, if not impossible, for the recruiter to find the most qualified candidate without helping you.

◆ You will tend to write more than you need to write because you're thinking that the extra tidbit you included (like bungee jumping off a bridge above the Amazon River in Brazil back in 1976) is the "hook" that will get you in the door. Don't. Unless you have irrefutable inside information, your reader is probably a) tired, b) dreading the prospect of seeing 2,000 resumes emailed/faxed/mailed to her/him when he/she is already too busy, c) under orders to find any excuse to pare the pile of resumes down to a manageable number, and d) is in the 99.9 percent group that does not care one iota that you were willing to risk killing or maiming yourself in the middle of the Amazon Basin 1,000 miles from civilization decades ago.

Instead, we recommend you make your cover letter brief, to the point and from the reader's point of view. Also ensure that the accomplishments you list in the cover letter can be found in your resume. Many times the two don't match, and as a result there is a disconnect between the resume and the cover letter.

Another approach to writing a cover letter specifically customized for the open position you are apply for is to make your cover letter look identical to the job description. If you can compare what they are looking for in a candidate with your own competencies and experiences, you have a better opportunity to attracting enough attention that may warrant an interview.

PERSONAL BUSINESS CARDS

Many people ask, "Why should I have a business card? I am out of work." Our response is that you are never out of work because you are always working for your MyPB. Company, and as such, you need a business card as a communications tool for your company. Questions to keep in mind about your personal business card:

1 Does it say something like "TJ Johnson, Finance" on the front? (If it does, you are one of the cans of soup perched behind the ones on the front part of the shelf because you have shown us no PCA.)

2 Did you put your email address on it? (Amazing how many business cards and resumes do not have one, which runs the risk of telling the person you are probably not equipped to deal with the technology world of the twenty-first century.)

3 Do you have your own website? (Websites are inexpensive to get, can provide you with a more professional email address, suggests you are more technology savvy [diluting the age issue], and can give you a way for the person you meet to easily go to your website and download your handbill, resume and maybe a paper you authored.)

4 Did you put anything on the back of the card? (Most people unfortunately choose not to use the free advertising space on the back to further market their product. On the other hand, avoid the temptation to put your entire resume on the back of the card.)

In summary, every job seeker needs to remember that:

1 You need a PCA to effectively compete in the race for your next job.

2 Your PCA needs to translate into a personal brand and become a component of a comprehensive, integrated personal marketing plan for your MyPB.

3 Develop a great resume and handbill.

4 Remember the listener's point of view when writing cover letters as well as all other correspondence.

5 Carry a personal business card at all times (put your brand on the card front and your tagline on the back of the card) because networking is a 24/7 commitment and opportunity.

6 Commit to having your own website to make it easy for people to get your marketing materials and to show you are tech savvy.

CHAPTER 4
NETWORKING & INTERVIEWING SKILLS

Becoming a successful job networker and interviewee will not come easily for many of you. Nevertheless, success as a job networker and interviewee is within your reach. If you have potential and are willing to work hard, you too can win the networking and interviewing portions of the race for your next job.

Your personal marketing preparation is now complete. You have already evaluated your personal executive strengths and weaknesses, completed RSAs (Results, Situation, Actions) to measure past accomplishments, written a narrowly focused and results-laden resume, and created a differentiating handbill, elevator speech and business card. Now you just have to go out there and get a job. So let's get in "shape" to actually run the job race… and win.

NETWORKING

Business job networking is the process of creating the opportunities to meet people in situations which may lead to additional opportunities to meet more people and/or identify a job or business opportunity. The initial networking we did in Gray Hair Management's early years, as well as the networking we continue to do today (GHM hosts job networking monthly events), taught us six things we recommend you will need to incorporate into your own job networking activities.

First, trust the statistics. There is a greater than 80 percent probability your next job opportunity will indeed result from someone you know, but that doesn't necessarily mean someone you know today. It could be someone you meet tomorrow.

Why does networking account for more than 80 percent of executive job placements? Part of the reason is because we also have learned that 72 percent of the people hired by companies are known to the companies in advance. What this means is that the new employee is usually referred to the company by another employee, a business associate or even a personal friend. Put these two statistics together, and it is easy to see why looking for a job is often a simple numbers game. The more people you know, the better the chance that you are going to hear about, and subsequently land, a new position.

Second, networking is a 24/7 activity, so you must practice it while being employed as well as when you are out of work. You never know when a planned meeting or chance introduction can lead to something job-related now or just down the road. So always be ready. We're amazed how often people we meet do not have a business card with them. One never knows when opportunity will knock. In fact, we have identified great networking opportunities at events ranging from weddings to bus rides.

Third, networking works best when you faithfully practice the axiom "you have to give in order to get." Great networkers have a mind set that always assumes you have to give in order to get. The five most important words in networking are "How can I help you?"

Networking, like good farming or smart investing, is a long-term commitment. As mentioned in an earlier chapter, we have adopted the adage that you have to give at least five times in order to receive something back. But that something you receive back may turn out to be something worth five times more than what you previously gave. Yes, giving can require a great deal of your time. Yes, you never know if or when you will start getting something back. Yes, there are a lot of opportunists out there who will be glad to take advantage of your generosity.

But those are the risks one must take in order to gain the full benefits of networking.

Business professionals need to get involved in many different types of events, including charitable foundations, college alumni associations, even political campaigns. One of our clients volunteered to personally contact all college alums who were invited to a 25 year reunion even though he had never previously helped his alma mater (great networking opportunity though). Another client volunteered to reorganize the entire office operation of a political candidate.

As each of you look back at your career to date, you have already had your share of good fortune, and it is never too late to start giving back. Giving (paying forward) is what networking is all about. If something great, like a job offer, also occurs by contributing to someone else, that's icing on the cake. If it does not occur, you still feel good about what you gave, and you still never know what may happen in the future when you continue to stay in touch with the people you help or try to help.

Fourth, networking requires great patience because it seldom gets results overnight. "Rome was not built in a day" is an old saying that applies to job networking as well. Good networking works on the pay-it-forward rule, which has no timetable. We're constantly amazed at the number of people we have met over the years who have subsequently referred business to us. We do not expect it, yet it happens. Your networking philosophy has to lack this timetable mentality as well. You may experience weeks, perhaps months of waiting for payback, and you begin wondering when this imprecise "science" of networking will pay off. Be patient. It does.

Fifth, networking is a great way to meet a lot of new, interesting people, so get out there and meet some interesting people. We sometimes equate job networking to playing the power ball lottery ... you cannot win unless you play. We are appreciative of the number of people we have met and continue to stay connected with over the years.

Sixth, we at GHM have identified three levels of job networking, "Takers" and "Givers" and "Connectors." The key to effective networking is to get to level three as quickly as possible.

Level one networkers are sometimes referred to as Takers. These people, despite good intentions, are unable to put their own personal business needs and goals aside to help others. Every meeting becomes an opportunity to first tell his/her story and to explain his/her needs. If someone asks this person early on in a conversation, "How can I help you?" the person is off to the races, talking the rest of the allotted time to fill you in on every detail of his/her situation and needs. When they do finish, they fail to ask, "Now that I have told you what I need, how can I help you?"

Level two networkers embrace and generally practice the concept that you have to give in order to get. They are Givers. Conversations with another individual more often than not result in a fairly balanced conversation (each person speaking half of the time). At the end of the conversation, this individual has successfully been able to learn quite a bit about the other person, and he/she has also asked, "How can I help you?" to the other party. Both parties involved in the conversation are generally satisfied with the meeting outcome.

Level three networking is where things really happen. These professionals really "get it" when it comes to giving in order to get. They become what we refer to as Connectors . . . professionals who will be remembered as "go to" networking resources after the meeting takes place.

How do you recognize a Connector? First, they get you to do over 70 percent of the talking. Second, the response to your question early in the conversation, "Tell me about yourself," takes less than 15 seconds for them to answer, and is quickly followed by an open-ended question directed back to you. Third, the "How can I help you?" question asked early on by you gets another less than 15 second response followed by another open-ended question directed back to you. Fourth, you feel guilty as the conversation comes to a close because you realize you have done most or all the talking. In fact, you feel so guilty that you may try to create more conversation time at the end of the meeting so you can finally learn more about that person. Marketing is about differentiating the product or service from the competition. Connectors understand this and successfully differentiate themselves from other networkers by being great listeners and by trying to help others.

So how does one become a Connector? Practice. Lots of it. When working with business professionals in job transition, we usually spend more time videotaping networking practice sessions than interviewing practice sessions. If one accepts the premise that there is an 80 percent probability that your next job will result from networking, then you have to make networking second nature. The way to do that is through lots of practice. And as you get better at being a Connector, you'll find you look more forward to attending planned and potential net-working group events as well as every one-on-one situation you encounter.

Successful job seekers also know how to use e-mail. The new economy has mandated that every employable person be capable of using e-mail effectively as a form of communications. A recent survey of recruiters indicated that there is an 85% preference to receive resumes by e-mail than by any other method. Adhering to these rules will increase your chances that the recruiter or prospective employer will read your resume.

1 Get a real e-mail address. Cutesy names like Slide2b@, Debbynooch@, hottotrot@, etc. tend to diminish the seriousness of your search. The closer your e-mail resembles your name, the better off you will be.

2 Don't share your e-mail address with members of your family. Get your own account with your own e-mail address. Sending a resume with your spouse's or family's return address is confusing and indicates that you may not possess the technological skills needed to communicate in today's economy.

3 Your resume and every other personal document should have your e-mail address included.

4 Your resume file should be a stand-alone attachment and not a zip file with several documents included. (Note: AOL generally "zips" all multiple attachments.)

5 Always make sure your full name is included in the resume file name you attach to your message. For example, "Kane_Scott_Resume.doc," and not "resume2001.doc." When the receiver copies your attachment to a folder, it will carry your name on it so that it can be easily retrieved.

6 If you're not using a mainstream word processing program (like MS Word), you will want to ensure that your document will open. You can do this by making it an .rtf file, or even a .txt file if you don't care about the formatting. Also, do not put your contact information into the header or footer. If a recruiter does not have his word processor set to read the "layout view," they will not see what's in the header and footer.

7 Always include a cover letter along with your full name and contact information in the body of the message. Don't include your cover letter as a second attachment with your resume for it will only confuse things.

8 Do not send your resume attached to a blank message. Because of the threat of a virus, it won't get opened or read.

9 Make sure that your reply address in your e-mail account is set up correctly, not only with your e-mail address, but your full name as well. You don't want replies to you to be undeliverable.

10 Treat and use your e-mail address as you would your own telephone number. In the not too distant future, it will become the more common method of contacting you.

Because there are three levels of networkers operating out there in the job marketplace, this is one of the reasons why many working executives are growing tired of being asked to network ... there are too many poor networkers. We need more Connectors out there!

We end the segment on networking with three great networking stories which demonstrate your need to "get in front of the bus" ... using your network to get to the hiring manager, and making a positive impact when you network. Tim, a senior executive with the sales credentials to be referred to as a CRO (Chief Revenue Officer), was out of work some years back. While driving in his car, he was slowed by some kind of traffic delay ahead of him, and traffic was at a standstill. While looking around, he noticed a limousine also stopped next to him. On an impulse, he rolled his window down and got the attention of the limo driver, who then rolled down his window. Tim requested that the limo driver ask the person in the back of the limo if he was interested in hiring a very good sales executive. The limo driver's window went back up, and traffic began moving again. A few minutes later, traffic came to a standstill, and Tim was again next to the limo. This time the limo driver's window went down, and he got Tim's attention. He then handed Tim a business card and said, "Call him on Monday." Tim made the call, and he in no time got a job. In fact, eight years later Tim had become president of that company, and he took it public. Now that is networking!

The second "getting in front of the bus" story comes from our own experience. We attended a senior networking meeting in downtown Chicago. One of our GHM Laws of Networking is "always meet the host or hostess of the event," so of course we went through the receiving line to meet the president of the group, a Fortune 100 CEO. With our regular GHM badges around our necks (and Scott leading the way), the CEO immediately noticed our unique company name and asked what GHM actually did. In addition to mentioning that we help senior executives such as this gentleman win the job race, we noted that senior executive jobs only last on average 1.8 to three years. So he smiled and promised to keep that information in mind.

Time passed. When we decided to go to that group's Christmas holiday networking event, we of course went through the receiving line. Guess who was in the receiving line and had lost his CEO position the month before the Christmas party event? You guessed it. We said hello, reminded him who we were (he remembered), and we suggested that perhaps we could help him. He agreed and after the start of the new year, we began a networking relationship that continues to this day.

Another executive was equally adept in terms of "getting in front of the bus." As the president of a men's clothing chain of retail stores closed down by their bank, this senior executive faced the prospects of perhaps not getting a job at the same level or even working again. He was having difficulty getting anyone to meet with him, let alone recognize his past accomplishments. He was convinced that if he were able to meet a decision maker, he was sure he could convince that decision maker that he could work for him. The executive created a strategy that included taking a part-time job in an Italian men's store in the Gold Coast section of Chicago, arguing that anyone who could afford a $250 tie was someone he wanted to meet. On Saturdays, he also took a part time job in an exclusive cigar store, arguing that anyone who could buy a $20 cigar was someone he wanted to meet. Over a period of time, one of his cigar store "regulars" and he got to know each other well. The "regular" subsequently asked him to come in and interview for a job in an industry in which our networker had no experience. He got a job and continues to work for this company. By finding a way to get in front of the bus, this executive proved that no matter what your long-time background has been, you can change industries.

As a matter of fact, we have found that of the senior manager we have in our GHM network who have found work, more than 60% have changed industries. How did they accomplish this when so many people tell us they are disqualified from positions because while they have wonderful credentials, they lack the specific experience in the market they are attempting to enter? In some cases, it was because the senior manager used his/her networking skills to get a meeting with the hiring manager and proved he/she was the best solution to the hiring manager's business problem. In other cases, they were able to establish a relationship contract with the hiring manager before a position was open. At a later date, the hiring manager's business then developed a problem; the manager thought of the networker as the possible solution to the problem, despite the person's different industry background, because he/she was now a known, competent performer.

INTERVIEWING

Most senior managers have probably done quite a bit of job interviewing during their business careers. That's the good news. If you are looking or thinking about looking for a new job, the bad news is that almost all of your experience has probably had you sitting in the wrong chair . . .the interviewer's chair.

So how do you increase your interviewing success rate? We suggest a three-step approach to better interviewing success: maintaining the right mental point of view; proper interview preparation; excellent interviewing techniques.

What is the correct interviewing mental point of view? Great interviewees recognize that an interview is really a sales presentation. The interviewer is the customer or prospect, and the interviewee is the salesperson selling his/her services to the interviewer's company. That means everything has to be approached from the interviewer's point of view. What we want as a job seeker should not be part of the initial interview preparation process. Instead, the key question we have to anticipate and respond to is "What's in it for me if I hire you?" Everything has to be based on the other person's point of view. If you can keep this key concept in mind preparing for and during each interview, your chances for success will immediately improve immensely.

Proper preparation for the interview is the second step to a successful interview. Here are five essentials we recommend you should do prior to an interview:

1 It (almost but not quite) goes without saying that you have to do your homework to learn about the company. Do a Google (or other search engine) search, read (if available) the annual report and/or 10K of the company when you can get them, tap into your network to see if anyone knows about the company or knows someone who knows something about the company. Leave no stone unturned to learn facts and corporate culture items about the company and its executives; then make that list of intelligent, probing questions you can ask during the interview to demonstrate your interest in the company as well as in the opportunity itself.

2 Make a list of the five toughest questions you could be asked, and write out answers to each question. This accomplishes two things. First, you have something to compare to the actual questions asked to see how well you anticipated what was going to be important to the interviewer(s). Second, you will be less nervous going into the interview if you have already addressed the tough questions. Here's a sample question: "I have five finalists for this position, and you are the only one without prior industry experience. Why should I hire you?" You may not have a great answer to that question, but formulating your answer before someone puts you on the interviewee hot seat will work out better for you.

3 Be sure you have written out your answers to at least seven questions (have a single 3x5 or 4x6 inch card for each so that these can also be used during a phone-screen interview as well as your one-on-one interviewee preparation). By having completed your RSAs, your resume, your handbill and your elevator speech, you should already have the answers to these seven questions:

a) Who are you? (Answer this question in less than 20 words based on the first part of your elevator speech.)

b) What is your personal competitive advantage over other candidates?

c) Can you tell me about a significant accomplishment that you are proud of? (Translate this so that you put a measurable result up front, not at the end, and try to link the accomplishment to the number one problem the person filling this job position will be asked to solve.)

d) How would someone who knew you very well professionally describe you to someone else?

e) What is your top business strength?

f) What is a skill or knowledge area where you are trying to improve?

g) How do you define great leadership?

The list can go on, but you get the idea… prepare.

4 When in doubt, dress business on the first interview. You can always take off a tie and/or a coat or jacket to quickly dress down a bit.

5 Be prepared to meet with good interviewers as well as bad interviewers. Top interviewers usually use a behavioral interview style (open-ended questions which can potentially lead anywhere because the interviewer is seeking repetitive behavior responses from the interviewee to identify and confirm behaviors). On the other hand, you may instead get interviewers who prefer asking planned, structured questions.

In either case, expect to do 80% of the talking and learning very little about the job position until the interviewer is satisfied that he/she "knows" you well. At that time, you'll get your chance to ask your questions and shift the conversation flow to more of a 50/50 (you talk, he/she talks) balance. But many poor interviewers will tend to do too much of the talking up front (could be good or bad for you), questions may tend to be close-ended ("Did you like your last job?" rather than, "What did you like and dislike about your last job?"), and questioning may seem very random. Part of the challenge of talking to an inexperienced interviewer is that you may not be able to "sell" the points you wish to convey that will differentiate you from the competition.

Inexperienced or poor interviewers also prejudge the candidate, making up their minds during the first few minutes of the interview and then justifying their decision the rest of the interview. So be especially prepared to be at the top of your game during the first 5-7 minutes of the interview.

There are several interviewing techniques that will improve your chances of success during an actual interview. These include maintaining strong eye contact with the interviewer, especially during the first 5-7 minutes of the interview. People often have a tendency to maintain good eye contact when the interviewer is doing the talking. Then, when asked a question, the interviewee's eyes are all of a sudden "searching the wall" while preparing to answer the question.

Do you do this? If you do, it is often because you personally feel embarrassed because you don't have an immediate answer to the person's question. So you look away for a moment until you prepare your answer. This perceived "lack of confidence" behavior can be rectified by remembering two things. First, it may seem "forever" to you when you are searching for that answer, but the fact is that it is usually less than a second (and you can fill in the short time gap by repeating or rephrasing the question while you look the person in the eyes and let your brain do its thing). Second, remember that the interviewer usually feels good when he/she asks you a "tough" question. Your pause can be a way of acknowledging "Tough question, way to go, let me dig for this one" in response to the good question asked by the interviewer. So it is okay to take less than a second to come up with an answer to a tough question (just do it without searching the wall or ceiling for the answer).

Avoid long, rambling initial responses that can confuse the interviewer. This can also make it difficult to allow the interviewer to stay in control of the conversation.

Instead, try to make a clear, cogent statement when you first respond, then briefly pause, and then be ready to go into more detail. That pause accomplishes two things. First, it gives the interviewer a chance to pick up on your comment and then either a) ask you to elaborate or b) change the subject if your answer was good enough. Second, it allows the point you initially made to be absorbed by the interviewer. If someone asks you about a major accomplishment, wouldn't you want to pause for impact if you had started your answer with "Geri, we were able to save the company $400,000 annually."?

Always interview as if you have a job. This is one of the lessons learned by many interviewees after the fact. We've learned that people out of work have a tendency to interview differently than when they were working. When out of work, the risk is that you end up feeling the extra pressure to get that job (either because you are desperate for a paid job, and/or you are just tired of being out of work) so much that you end up pushing too hard to get the job. In order to avoid this, you have to remind yourself that you are never out of work. Yes, you may not be receiving a W2 for the time being, but you are still employed by your company, My Personal Business. It is critical to remember this because it increases your chances of being more patient during the interview process. Why? Having a job gives you added structure (structure was discussed in an earlier chapter), and that added structure enables you to deal from a position of strength: employment. So give yourself the same edge current W2-receiving competitors for that job you are seeking have … the security of employment.

Have some fun, and smile once in a while during the interview. Part of your strategy during an interview is to form a relationship contract (remember that phrase from an earlier chapter?) with the person sitting across from you. Your personality needs to come through as well as your commitment to work hard and accomplish great results. Remember that you are being evaluated in five major areas: knowledge, skills, behavior factors, corporate culture fit and compatibility with the new manager. For many jobs, 80% of job success after the initial screening is a function of interpersonal chemistry. Create some chemistry and relax.

Remember that "perfect practice makes perfect." Consequently, practice early and often. We cannot emphasize enough the need for you to do a lot of videotape practice. The difference between getting or not getting a job offer can be as little as two percent (you being two percent better or worse than your competitor), so find the extra two percent to make yourself a better interviewee.

Whether you need a personal mentor or coach (like the 1980 American hockey team did and every successful professional athlete uses) or whether you can do this all on your own, one of the keys to winning the race for your next job is to leverage your personal integrated marketing package by becoming a great Connector and interviewee. Since there is no money for second place in an interview situation, train yourself with only one goal in mind: winning.

More than anything else, commit to finding the best way to leverage your talents in this race for your next job. If that means doing things a little differently than you are used to doing them, be sure you get good advice from people you trust, and have the confidence to make those changes. If your job search strategy does not seem to be working for you, you may want to look outside your current group of advisors and consider some coaching help. Find that extra two percent that can make the difference in your job search success.

CHAPTER 5

BUILDING THE KNOW NETWORK^{sm}

Building a personal network of contacts is an essential part of your long-term success in building your career. We assume you are committed to being a great Connector as defined in chapter four. This chapter will give you some suggestions how to build and maintain a network. We call it your Know Network^{sm}.

BUILDING YOUR KNOW NETWORK

First, decide on the size of your Know Network. How many people do you need to have in your network to be assured that you will have adequate connections the next time you will have to look for a job? One great Connector we know well has over 400 people in his network. When he lost his last position as CEO of a well known US company, he was able to use his network to land his next job while he was still negotiating his severance and outplacement package with his soon-to-be ex employer. How? He had a lot of friends helping him... his Know Network.

Most business professionals probably have less than 75 people in their networks. Based on our experience working with professionals in transition, it is our opinion that senior managers need to have at least 200 people in their personal network. Why so many? You never know who is going to be the person who will help you identify your next opportunity, so the more friends you have, the better. Since people are changing jobs and moving at an increasing pace, you can lose 5-7% of your network in any given year without even trying. The time required to initially establish that number of contacts and then maintain that many network contacts is not easy. Your mission here is to establish yourself as a go-to person, as a person ready and willing to help other people whenever possible. The ultimate size of your network depends on your discipline as a Connector to stay connected with these people. Bottom line: your future career success and financial well being depend on it.

Second, you also need to organize your network. We have seen very good networkers using a variety of database management systems to keep track of their contacts. Systems range from the simple (Excel spread sheet or four-by-six inch cards) to the sophisticated (ACT, Goldmine, Outlook). The one thing they all have in common is the ability to help you prioritize contacts so you can follow up accordingly.

We suggest you create three groups of contacts based on frequency of contact: inner circle (contact every 90 days, preferably face-to-face whenever possible), middle circle (contact twice a year, usually by phone) and then the "Christmas" circle (contact once a year, usually by email). Visually, think of it as a series of concentric circles with you in the middle circle surrounded by your Know Network. Around you is a circle initially segmented by the groupings you create to separate your contact types. For example, one client successfully separated contacts by either being family/friends, executive search, sales, marketing, operations, administration, or other. Another way of breaking people into segments can be by distribution versus manufacturing versus services. The "best" way is the way that is easiest for you to manage. Your next circle consists of your inner circle (90 day) names followed by your middle circle (twice a year) names and, finally, by your Christmas circle (once a year) names.

An example of the My Know Network appears on the opposite page depicting the executive search contacts for an individual broken down by the number of times each executive should be contacted annually.

My Know Network℠ Format

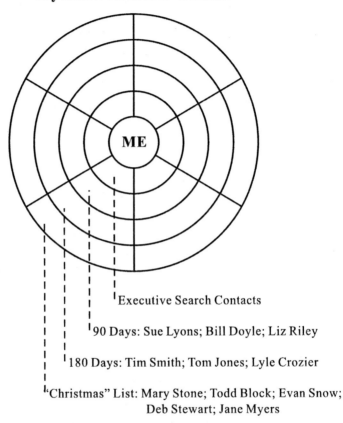

Executive Search Contacts

90 Days: Sue Lyons; Bill Doyle; Liz Riley

180 Days: Tim Smith; Tom Jones; Lyle Crozier

"Christmas" List: Mary Stone; Todd Block; Evan Snow; Deb Stewart; Jane Myers

Third, every quarter you should update your contacts, adding names, deleting names and moving contact names closer or farther away from you depending upon the value of connecting with each person.

Fourth, finalize how you are going to stay connected with your three rings of contacts. In most cases, your 90 day circle will be the people you are going to meet with face-to-face as often as possible. When you cannot meet them personally, you will probably want to at least be calling them every quarter. The 180 day circle of contacts will most likely be contacted through a combination of phone calls and personal emails. As we noted earlier, the Christmas circle list is most likely just an email away every year. If possible, you want to try to break this group into four sub-groupings over time so that you contact a fourth of them each quarter. That way you do not run the risk of saying hello to all these people at the same time, then losing your job 11.5 months later. Make sense?

Fifth, try to start building up your network when you are working. For all you business executives still working out there, your out-of-work counterparts will all tell you they should have started building their Know Network while they were working too.

Sixth, attend as many group meetings as possible. Look for opportunities and excuses to go to conferences, transition meetings (even when you are working), anywhere you have a chance to meet new people as well as renew old acquaintances. Leverage your time.

Seventh, volunteer and take advantage of changes in your business that gives you an excuse to contact people. One of our clients interested in seeking a new opportunity moved office sites. This became a great opportunity to contact everyone imaginable to notify them of the move (lots of follow up breakfasts and lunches as he used this as an excuse to connect).

Eighth, decide how much time you are going to spend each month networking, and keep your commitment. Networking is a critical time commitment you must make to your MyPB personal business. If you choose to ignore this responsibility and instead get too wrapped up in only working for your "other" employer, you place yourself at significant job loss risk.

TRACKING YOUR NETWORKING EFFORTS

The management axiom "that which gets measured gets done" applies to networking. For anyone who is out of work looking for a job or for anyone working who is trying to get a new job as soon as possible, one of the challenges they face is falling onto the trap of thinking that they only have one goal: get a job. This kind of thinking causes two problems. First, it is a false assumption because it ignores other critical goals such as the need to build your personal Know Network, and the need to continue developing your business skills. Second, it increases the risk that you will misallocate how you are spending your time as you look for your next job opportunity.

Our experience with our own out of work mentoring clients confirms that that many of them have great difficulty staying focused doing the activities they must do to get that next opportunity. Our experience with our own working mentoring clients who are also actively looking for a job confirms that many of them also have difficulty making the time to perform the activities they must do to get that new job opportunity (they get too busy doing their W2 job to have time for MyPB activities).

In either situation, the key becomes identifying the job search activities that should be measured, developing goals for each activity, and then measuring levels of success in achieving those goals. You can do your tracking on an Excel spread sheet. For example, in the first column, list the activities you want to measure.

Your list might include:

1 Attend group networking meetings I (primarily transition executive attendees).

2 Attend group networking meetings II (primarily working executive attendees).

3 Conduct one-on-one networking meetings (by phone).

4 Conduct one-on-one networking meetings (face-to-face).

5 Send out fishing (unsolicited) letters.

6 Respond to job postings.

7 Obtain phone screening interviews.

8 Obtain face-to-face job interviews.

Next to each activity in the second column, write down your weekly target goals. For example, you might strive for one (transition) networking meeting, two (working) networking meetings, two phone network meetings, five face-to-face network meetings, three fishing letters, three job postings, one phone screen and one face-to-face job interview.

In each subsequent column, keep track of how many actual accomplishments you had each week (for fishing letters and for responses to job postings, we suggest you also keep track of how many responses you get). After three or four weeks, evaluate results, and change goals and/or change activity effort accordingly to improve performance results. You can make the sheet as complicated as you want. The key is to meet or exceed your goals. Job search often becomes a numbers game... doing enough of the right things enough times to generate a job offer.

CHAPTER 6
WINNING THE CAREER RACE

You are now ready to effectively run the job race in order to get the most out of your business career. Knowing your strengths, weaknesses, career accomplishments... ready. Second-to-none resume, handbill, elevator speech, business cards, killer letters... ready. Skilled network builder, network manager, Connector, interviewee... ready. Go get that next great job opportunity!

NEGOTIATING THE JOB OFFER

We have learned that the degree to which you can successfully negotiate a job offer varies greatly. For example, one senior technology officer coaching client was able to successfully link the financial values of his accomplishments at his previous positions (in a different industry) to the expected financial value of contributions at his new company sufficiently to negotiate a 30% increase in starting salary. On the other hand, we have clients who have gotten "take or leave it" offers, and the company really meant it.

Because there are already so many books discussing the art of using time, information and power in negotiations, we chose to limit our remarks on job negotiation to the four critical negotiating tips that have benefited our coaching clients the most. They are:

1 Avoid negotiating anything until you get an official offer in writing. We have seen too many verbal offers go up in smoke because executives started to negotiate points in the verbal offer. In fact we have received stories about job offers being withdrawn.

2 Define the point where you are prepared to end the negotiation and walk away from the job offer before you negotiate anything. Job negotiations (assuming you can negotiate) are not like extended union labor contract negotiations or the drawn out war negotiation with the North Vietnamese years ago. In this case you have a very short time window of opportunity.

3 Try to start any job negotiation by letting the hiring manager know up front that you are moving ahead with the intention of wanting to become an employee of the company. Your actions must be viewed by the hiring manager as a win/win rather than win/lose strategy. Keep it positive.

4 Make sure you understand the hiring manager's COS (conditions of satisfaction). Try to get in writing what it is that will demonstrate to the hiring manager (and to you) what needs to occur within a stated time period (let's say your first six and first twelve months on the job) in order for that manager to be satisfied that you are successfully doing the job. Remember that so much of an executive's success on the job is based as much on chemistry between the manager and the executive as it is on the actual efforts and results of the newly hired executive. Understand the COS.

STAYING IN CONTROL
OF YOUR CAREER

We also recommend that you start planning to do one more thing. Write up a Personal Business Plan for your MyPB company. This becomes your personal plan to follow as soon as you get that next job opportunity. GHM developed a template for our mentoring clients (we coach our clients when they are actively looking for their next job opportunity, we mentor our clients when they are working) to use when they have landed and are ready to go on a quarterly meeting schedule with GHM. We developed it to resemble a modified SWOT (strengths, weaknesses, opportunities and threats) Analysis used by many businesses during corporate strategic planning combined with a strategic vision of where you want to be combined with a quarterly list of goals to accomplish. The format appears here:

GHM CLIENT NAME
GHM CLIENT PERSONAL BUSINESS PLAN
DATE:

PART ONE: STRATEGIC GOALS

1 Describe where you need to be in terms of personal wealth, career satisfaction, recognition in the community and anything else that will indicate you have successfully reached the "end point" of your Personal Business Plan journey.

2 In what year do you want to be in that "end point" position?

3 Describe the final job position you need to be in prior to reaching your "end point" position.

4 Identify the major obstacle you will need to overcome in order to reach your "end point." (If that obstacle is not knowing what your final job position will be, then go to the Career Options Analysis Section below and complete that section.)

PART TWO: SITUATION ANALYSIS

1 List your personal strengths.
(Helpful to refer to your Need-Press Analysis Profile results.)

2 List your personal development opportunities.
(Helpful to refer to your Need-Press Analysis Profile results.)

3 Define your work "passion."

4 What work activities do you avoid doing the most?

5 Define job "success."

6 Current job balance sheet.

   a. Company name:
   b. Position title:
   c. Major job duties:
   d. Best Aspects of Job:
   e. Job deficiencies and/or questions to resolve:

7 My Personal Know Network℠ status list.

   a. Contact every 90 Days: #
   b. Contact every 180 Days: #
   c. Christmas list: #
   d. Total: #

PART THREE: NEXT QUARTER GOALS AND TACTICS

1 Describe your strategy to improve your number one personal development activity to improve your performance.

2 List your next quarter job goals and any additional non-network goals you will be working on this quarter.

3 List any goals that will turn into RSAs.

4 List your personal network goals (additions) and the activities you need to do to achieve them.

5 Review the other parts of your Personal Business Plan for any other changes.

PART FOUR: CAREER OPTIONS ANALYSIS

1 Omitting your current job "space," what are other career paths you might consider?

2 What questions do you want answered about each career option?

3 Who are you going to meet to learn about those other career options?

4 What are the trends/forecasts of each career option?

5 Add anything you need to do next quarter to Part Three above.

Each person can make the plan as brief or as comprehensive as needed in order for them to move forward with direction and with a measuring tool. The Personal Business Plan should be updated quarterly, which provides the business professional a chance to review and revise the plan as needed with a business coach and/or with the person's personal board of advisors.

Does anything typically go wrong with the quarterly plan accomplishments? Yes. First, developing new RSAs is doable, although the results you expected to accomplish when you started working at a new job can be difficult to complete. The reason is often because many times the problem described by the hiring manager prior to your being offered a job becomes a problem the hiring manager subsequently chooses to ignore.

If this happens to you, you must seriously consider whether or not the job you got will hurt your chances of getting a subsequent job. The reason is because you may not be able to generate good enough RSAs to enable you to effectively compete against others for your next opportunity. If it does hinder you, you may want to seriously begin thinking about looking for a new job while you are working. Always remember: the best time to look for a job is when you are working.

There is a second problem that is even more likely to occur. When executives are out of work, one of the things they almost always discover is that they had been so busy working they did not have time to adequately identify and form new relationships to add to their own personal network. (In fact, they also did not have time to connect with old friends and associates in their existing network.) Having discovered that reality after being out of work, they promise to rectify that earlier error on their part and be a great network builder for the rest of their business career. Great. And then they get a job. Ninety days later we are getting ready to do our first quarterly meeting with the now-working client. One of our questions (part of the Personal Business Plan quarterly assignment): "So how did you do adding to your personal network of executives?" The answer: "Gee, Jack, I have been so busy working that I really haven't had time to do much networking. But I promise to get started in earnest next quarter." You can probably guess what happens when the next quarterly meeting happens. Yep. Same thing. So we spend a great deal of time helping each executive figuring out how to find enough time to network. Avoid letting this happen to you. Networking has to continue as an ongoing activity for the rest of your business career.

CHAPTER 7
SUCCESS IS PACKAGED IN MANY WAYS

It's a great feeling to get a call or an e-mail from one of our mentoring clients or from one of our GHM network members telling us they got a job. We started getting "landing notices" (e-mail announcements usually describing the position obtained and the way the person was able to land the job) shortly after GHM got started. Starting in 2002, we formalized the landing process because we felt it would be beneficial to all of our GHM members to pass on those landing notices in the hope each member's success formula for finding a job might help other members. In addition, we wanted to let executives know there were jobs out there in what often seemed a barren job market place.

SUCCESS CASE STUDIES

In 2002 and 2003 GHM received over 1,500 landing announcements. We still continue this practice of tracking landings today. We decided to include some of the more interesting landing e-mails we have received from GHM members as part of our closing chapter. We hope they give you some insights as well as some confidence as you continue along your personal pathway through career transition. Our thanks to those members who shared. Here they are:

E-Mail 1

After 435 days, seven seasons, two gardens, eight haircuts and 235 job applications I have finally landed a

VP/CIO position and I owe it all to Gray Hair Management (or a couple of fortune cookies).

Back in April my best friend and I went out to a Chinese joint in Palatine and my fortune said, "An outstanding opportunity will soon present itself to you."

On the following Monday I received a call from Jeff at Gray Hair and after a pretty good screening he promised me that I would receive a call from some secret company in the following week. I didn't know what day or what time and I didn't know what company but I was assured that I was going to get a call.

The entire week went by and I received no call. Disappointed, my best friend and I were preparing to go out to another cheap Friday night dinner to celebrate our 22nd wedding anniversary when the phone rang at 6:30 pm - I finally got the call, the initial interview, and another interview scheduled for the following week. By eight o'clock that night we were excited about the late phone interview and we were off to our next Chinese dinner.

"Next month shall be hectic, yet delightful".

What a fortune and what a job! (VP/CIO for The Gingiss Group) The following month was surely hectic and absolutely delightful! (I still have both fortunes taped to my home office monitor).

Having a job, in these harsh economic times, is a miracle all by itself and I know that I am especially lucky. My commute is a fraction of what it used to be, I didn't have to move to New Jersey or Sidney Nebraska, I work with the best team that I have ever seen throughout my career and the company cleans my shirts each week for free!

Thank you Gray Hair! Thank you Jeff and Scott and Jack!

Thank you, Debbie – for fulfilling your 22-year-old contract obligations – "through good times and bad times".

(And thank you……fortune cookies).

Sincerely,

Ray Costello

E-Mail 2

After 22 months of imminent and actual unemployment (actually 39 months, interrupted by ten months as associate university counsel for health care at UIC), I'm delighted and relieved to tell you that I have landed.

Beginning December 29th, I will be General Counsel for ZT Technical Services, LLC in Arlington Heights, Illinois as well as for its sister company, HTZ Technical Services, Inc. in Boca Raton, Florida. Formed in 1999, ZT Technical Services (ZT are the initials of the owner's first two children, Zack and Talia) is the nation's largest in-office electrodiagnostic testing company, specializing in neurological testing by technicians that see the patient in their doctor's office. HTZ Technical Services (the owner's third child is named Hayley) provides in-office neurodiagnostic testing services targeted to the chiropractic profession. ZT has revenues of about $70 million.

As it turned out, I learned about ZT on the Internet through Careerbuilder.com. However, for the past three months, I've been working on a contract basis in the legal department of TAP Pharmaceutical Products, Inc., and that virtually life-sustaining position came through some long-term networking that worked. Over 15 months ago, the husband of someone who was on the Ravinia Nursery School board with my wife 15 years earlier shared with me the name of a former co-worker in the United Airlines legal department who now works at TAP. He forwarded my resume to TAP's General Counsel, who had nothing available but said he'd "save my resume in his file". Well, we all know what that means. Amazingly, 13 months later, he contacted me about an opening for a contract attorney, which I filled this past October. So do not underestimate the long-term, incremental impact of networking, and don't be surprised at where leads come from.

I want to thank everyone who helped me during this extended period, by offering me contacts, being a wise sounding board, and generally helping me move forward against what at times was a pretty strong current. I will do my best to remain active with the group, and would be happy to help anyone in any way I can.

Rick Hinden

E-Mail 3

Ten months after the end of my previous assignment, I am pleased to report I have landed a new position as Managing Director of an industrial distribution company in Taiwan. Most of my life I have worked internationally in the heavy equipment industry and the position is the kind of work I was looking for.

My search process was quite traditional, distributing my credentials to the major recruiting firms and networking my contacts. In addition, I paid a well-known firm to mail out about 15,000 resumes, and I can say now that it was a complete waste of time and money. In this modern era, about 90% of the communications are electronic. Mailed resumes usually do not even make it past the screeners. The only responses I got were requests to send the information electronically. I believe it is important to have a personal web site and to use the various methods of modern electronic communication systems. One must be able to demonstrate good computer literacy, including not only the common PC applications, but also knowledge of the Internet and networking systems, etc. Know the buzzwords, and what they mean. Otherwise, an older person is 'dead in the water'. It may be interesting to point out that I did my search first while in the Bahamas, then while cruising on my boat for six months (wireless connectivity is easy these days), and then for a period of time while in Canada. GHM was present throughout the journey, even though I was nowhere near Chicago.

There is no doubt that my age was a significant handicap in the search process (63 years young), and yet this can be overcome with the right attitude and being able to demonstrate physical and mental energy. Stay active and keep fit. For those of us who are age-handicapped, it is also necessary to clearly communicate the benefits of one's experience and maturity. That is, one must not only talk about what one has done, but more importantly, be able to show specifically why it will be beneficial to a particular employer. Showing future promise may work for others, but not for us older folks. You must hit the ground running because the honeymoon period will be very short.

Best regards,
Maurice Marwood
mmarwood@mmarwood.com

E-Mail 4

Dear Jack & Scott,

I am delighted to report I have recently landed as a consultant with The Entrepreneur's Source. This is a franchise opportunity where I will use my skills as an entrepreneur, coach, and businessperson to help mid-career professionals identify their goals, needs and expectations and to find business-ownership opportunities that fulfill them.

At this point in my ongoing GHM Pathways process, I want to pause to thank you both for all your help in getting me to this point. During the past year we have worked together, I have come to know my own skills and unique abilities much more clearly. This gives me the confidence to network and effectively market myself (VP

Marketing for Charlie Scarlett Corp!), and to try different challenges. I have also come to value the GHM process. It has given me an appreciation for the continuing, lifelong process and the tenacity to stick with it. It works!

I come from a mid-sized business background – the senior executive for "wings, wheels & rudders" (thank you Scott!). I have run businesses successfully for others for my entire career. Completing a number of consulting gigs during this past year, I realized I no longer want the corporate life. So I decided to go into business for myself. Choosing a franchise reduced the risk. Business format franchising enables me to be in business with a proven system — in business FOR myself, but not BY myself. I truly appreciate the benefits and flexibility of being my own boss. It's still hard work, but it's MY work – and much more rewarding.

GHM has unleashed my ability to network effectively and market my unique skills. I believe in the process. It has worked for me and I believe it will continue to work for me throughout my career. As Spencer Johnson pointed out so eloquently in <u>Who Moved My Cheese?</u>, change is the only constant and its pace is increasing. It can be a blessing or a curse. GHM has helped me effectively embrace change and pursue its blessings.

Thanks Jack & Scott! I look forward to your continuing coaching.

> Cheers,
> Charlie Scarlett

E-Mail 5

I am happy to report that I have landed! A couple of months ago I accepted a position with Accenture as an experienced consultant. The work is challenging and demanding and very hectic. But I am learning something new every day and I am grateful to be back with the "working class".

Current job seekers please take note: I received the job lead from the Gray Hair Management email postings. I responded and it took about nine months to finally land the job. I didn't give up and stayed in touch with the recruiter even though it looked, at times, like my employer was no longer interested in my resume.

To those who say age is a barrier, I say "not if you let it." I am of the gray hair age group but try not to let it show. I keep my appearance, attitude and energy level up. This is especially important when interviewing for a job. You will be perceived how you act. Act young and vibrant and you will be perceived as younger than you are and enthusiastic in your outlook. Employers want enthusiastic people who are interested and can bring fresh ideas to the job.

Scott, let me add my sincere "Thank-you" to you and the others who created the Gray Hair Management network. The articles, emails, job leads, inspiration and hope you bring to folks who are out of work are a godsend.

Please keep me on your list. I will do what I can to help others who are still out of work.

Sincerely,
Name withheld

E-Mail 6

Dear GHM Members:

I just wanted to let you all know that after approximately two years of networking and consulting, I landed in late July but have waited until now to publish the news.

I accepted the Director of Distribution position with a small but rapidly growing scrapbooking company called Making Memories, Inc. in Salt Lake City, Utah. My contact information is shown below so to all my friends, drop me an electronic note or give me a call and let me know what you are doing and how can I help you.

During my time in transition I have read some amazing and eloquent "landed monologs," and I won't even attempt to reiterate the amazing lessons and networking skills I've learned, nor to thank the countless number of good friends and total strangers who have taken their time to help me, but thank you anyway.

My story is simple but demonstrates that we all need networking contacts at some time or other, now or in the landed afterlife. I needed a contact at Fiskars in Madison, Wisconsin to follow-up on a job I was pursuing. Dick Stoller, a fellow networker, answered my request for information and gave me a name. The Fiskars thing went nowhere, but I established a relationship with the contact person. We talked and E-mailed each other a few times with advice and networking assistance.

A few months later, the contact person in Madison accepted the CEO position with Making Memories, Inc. and needed a strong Distribution & Logistics guy (me) to lead the Distribution technology upgrade and customer fulfillment areas of this rapidly growing scrapbook wholesaler. Scrapbooking is now the 3RD largest craft activity in the U.S., so take a peek at our website at www.makingmemories.com and get your wife hooked on this neat activity so I can have more job security.

Long story short, the job is great, the Salt Lake area is phenomenally beautiful ("best skiing in the US" according to the locals) and some fantastic Harley riding to feed my mid-life crisis habit; so life is good.

Now, I would like to stay connected and help any GHM members that I can, so please contact me and I will try to get in touch as soon as my schedule will allow. Try either the home or work E-mail and I will help you if I can.

> Best of luck to all.
> Bill Lenkowski

E-Mail 6

In February, 2002, my position as VP of International Sales was eliminated after nearly 7.5 years of employment in the Philly area. At the time, I was 62 years old.

Through significant networking, I learned of a new position whereby I could work as a virtual Eastern Region Sales Executive for a Milwaukee based systems' integration company. Following three interviews over a 30 day period, I was selected and started in May, 2002. I was landing #142. After 16 months of hard work, that position was also eliminated – much to my surprise.

The best news of all is that, again through networking, I learned (through a fellow church member) of a small local company interested in expanding. Following three long meetings over a period of eight (8) days, we finalized on the terms of an employment agreement. This all took place in eleven (11) days which was totally amazing.

This may be the best opportunity of all looking back over my 40+ year career in the AutoID industry sector.

SSI, Inc. is in the business of providing OEM Equivalent print heads (and select other parts) for thermal bar code label printers. We are planning on significant worldwide growth over the next 3 – 5 years. If you know of companies that use large quantities of label printers, we would appreciate being forwarded contact details of the decision maker for their replacement print head purchases.

I want to once again thank GHM for this incredible networking service. I still read every message each day and have been able to help a number of people. For those of you still searching for that new position, I can only suggest "KEEP THE FAITH" and always answer the phone as if the person on the other end is about to offer you that ideal new job.

I am reminded by a seminar given by Zig Ziglar, who ended his motivational "See You at the Top" message with "It is not your Aptitude but your Attitude that will determine your Altitude".

If I can be of help to any of you, please feel free to contact me at any time.

Good Luck,
Jack Householder

E-Mail 7

I found a position that is a great fit.

As of this past May 27th I assumed the position of President/COO of Bomarko, Inc. Bomarko is a paper, film and foil converter in NW Indiana. We service the confectionery, medical packaging and consumer products industries. Bomarko is a specialty converter with 250 employees and three facilities.

I'm in the middle of a restructuring program and will be on target to complete the first phase near the end of this year. The business has a fabulous niche and we'll expand it as we move forward in the coming years. Some of our customers include Wrigley's, Cadbury, J&J, and dozens of companies in the candy, gum and medical bandage-wrapping industries. All of my executive staff (including Operations, Sales and Finance) is over 50 years of age, and I'm fortunate for their experience levels to support my initiatives.

I will be commuting for some time, but the company has many customers in the Chicagoland area. So I will also work out of my home office. This opportunity satisfies many of my criteria of a company in transition, it is in the printing/converting/packaging industry, over $50 million/year in sales and, most importantly, it has tremendous growth potential in the industries we are in. Finding the environment where I could develop a long term relationship was also critical.

As many landed members have described their journey, I too had a varied and at times painful process. I have implemented almost every process to maintain a search including mail campaigns, recruiters, direct contacts and of course - networking. I am very computer literate and developed a massive database of contacts. However, it was always networking and personal references that made the difference.

At the beginning of this year, I involved myself in supporting new members of a job networking group I participated in doing peer reviews, and it was during this process that I met Frank Mayer. Working with him on his review, he mentioned that he was interviewing at Bomarko but felt that the position would not be a fit due to the required traveling. He suggested that I should look at it and at first I negated it also, largely because of the traveling, but decided to have a closer look.

After several interviews, visits to Bomarko offices and negotiations, I accepted the position. I am at Bomarko now because Frank Mayer placed me into the company's line of candidates. My experience and skill sets contributed to my hire but networking connected us. A big "thank you" to you Frank!!!

I will continue my membership in GHM and a few other groups - not only to be current with other managers but also to have a pipeline for management resources that I'll need to build Bomarko. I also extend my support to members for any help in their search.

I am extremely grateful to all the people that made this journey bearable, and I will never forget the process.

ll attempt to attend some of the GHM meetings in the next several weeks and will look forward to sharing any help to the members.

Géza J. Verik

E-Mail 8

After what seems like an eternity I have landed quite a nice position with International Truck and Engine Company in Warrenville, Illinois.

I am a Supply Chain Manager in the Truck Division. After taking an enhanced separation offer from Lucent 2 years ago I have had a handful of bad to awful "jobs". I do have a couple of words of advice based on my experiences over the past two years which I believe maps with the mission of GH. I hope this will help fellow member to stay out of some of the traps I fell into.

1) Keep the email searches on the job boards down to a maximum of 2 hours per day. Do look at the boards 7 days a week.

2) Never trust a headhunter unless you know them personally. They have a vested interest in themselves. Many companies refuse to work with them.

3) Recognize that finding a good position is secondary to maintaining your confidence and self esteem during this stressful period. Keep your head up. You have a lot of very qualified company these days. If needed take a "job" but continue to look for what you want. This temporary job offers new networking opportunities.

4) Decide what your strengths are and what type of function/role you would see yourself in 3-5 years from now. Research target companies which map with this objective and look for those companies/industries on the upswing. Do not "pigeon hole" yourself by previous industry or background experiences.

5) Do not "shotgun" it looking for a position. Invest the time necessary to research companies and make every communication count.

6) The hard part - NETWORK. No one will find a job for you other than yourself. GHM was very helpful in

breaking my mindset that a job will come to me because I am qualified. The GHM sessions in Lombard were very helpful as was the email network. Use your networking contacts to get you to the target hiring manager and to best help prepare for the interview(s) to come. Remain confident throughout the interviewing process. This step was key to my successful placement.

I will continue to watch the requests for information and provide assistance where possible. I will never forget the willingness of strangers to help me. I wish all the best in their career search.

Sherwin Gilbert

E-Mail 9

I want to add my name to those who have landed a position recently. I did not immediately announce my new position because I wanted to make sure it was for real. After ten months in transition in this lousy economy, I did not want to take anything for granted. However, after six weeks in my new position, I feel compelled to thank you and GrayHairManagement.com for being one of two keys that opened doors for me through networking. Between your organization and that of Laurie Rosen's JVS weekly network group, I finally achieved the goal I had set for myself.

You may recall that I have an extensive hospitality and travel background, but wanted to re-create myself into an industry that had not been so badly affected by 9/11 and an industry that has a future. You may also recall that I wanted to get into the senior living, or assisted living industry as the job qualifications greatly parallel my service industry and people centric skills.

I had targeted Sunrise Senior Living amongst several others and was having no luck. Until....one day I joined GrayHairManagement.com, wrote an email message describing my skill sets and listed target companies.

Imagine my surprise when a gentleman by the name of Greg Vos emailed me back within a very short time with invaluable information. He knew the Senior VP Human Resources for Sunrise and asked me to forward him my resume. To make a long story short, from that moment on, I was contacted by Sunrise and went through an extensive interview process. I was offered a position as an Executive Director (first in training as an Associate Executive Director) and started the position in mid-July.

As I have told everyone I meet who is in similar circumstances to me, get on-line and access GrayHairManagement.com. I only wish I had known about it early in my search as I am convinced I would have been employed much sooner. I want to thank you for making this connection possible through networking. I look forward to being of service to someone else in the future.

Thank you so much.
Michael Krause

E-Mail 10

I wanted to let you know that I've officially landed at Crowe Chizek and Company LLC., as Editor-in-Chief of Thought Leadership. My office is in Oak Brook, Illinois.

For the past 20 years, I have specialized in customer-facing operations/strategies (CRM, Sales, Marketing, A/R), focusing on start-ups and reorganizations in several industry verticals and almost any size company. During GHM networking events, I proudly communicated that I was looking for a VP/Chief Customer Officer position, here in the Chicagoland area.

I was laid-off from my global position at Arthur Andersen April 2002 after having been there only two years. Several of Andersen's Partners went to other consulting firms, and of course I stayed in touch with as many of them as I could. During the summer of 2002, two Partners completed a deal with Crowe and started Crowe's first Risk Management practice. I really enjoyed working with those two Partners at Andersen, so I voluntarily sent them updates on CRM Risk, Sarbanes-Oxley, leads and contacts for new business development, etc. Crowe had interest in hiring me in a Strategic Business Unit (SBU) not related to the Risk team, I went through two very successful interviews and because I didn't bring a book of business with me, I did not get a job offer (meaning that the SBU that had wanted to hire me - CRM client delivery – couldn't because they could not justify another FTE without more client work to offset it).

I was about to give up and live in an ashram somewhere very remote. A couple of networking people gave me some very good advice; stay in touch with them and don't give up until they say 'no'. Well, Crowe hadn't said 'no', they just said we can't figure out a way to get you here - yet.

So, after a few days of licking my wounds, I picked myself up - for what seemed like the hundred thousandth time in my life - and I stayed in touch with those two Partners. I completely took my ego out of the process, stayed proud and stood up straight. (I also gardened at a manic pace.)

In September 2002, Crowe expressed an interest to bring me on as a part-time contractor, creating CRM Risk Management tools for those two Partners and then to leverage those tools across the entire Firm. It wasn't until November that we finally shook hands and consummated the deal.

I worked from November 2002 through March 2003 on that project (along with several other projects that came my way), AND I networked like crazy inside the Firm. My contract was to end April 1, 2003.

During the second week of April, I was having a regularly scheduled project update meeting with my Partner in Michigan. We were winding my project and contract down and during that conversation, I expressed an idea that just sort of came to me. I told him that Crowe should consider writing some bylined articles for publication and/**or** delivering white papers out of the materials that the Risk Management Partners had already created. Well, that was my defining moment.

I did not realize that Crowe had been thinking about formalizing Thought Leadership and Knowledge Management for over a year, and had been having a difficult time developing a strategy, let alone find the right person to do this sort of work.

Because I had done some writing and KM work at Andersen, and because of the communication skills I unconsciously exhibited while working on my part-time contract, I was offered the permanent position as Editor-in-Chief within one week of that fateful conversation. I created my own job description and as of April 1, 2003, I landed.

During the past four months, this program has taken off like wildfire. I am so very swamped and Crowe's executives are excited about being able to present their skills and talents in well respected publications. I am now about to expand the program.

Is this a mid-life career change? I don't know! It sure seems to me that I'm using all of the same skills and talents that I used in previous jobs - leading, writing, analyzing, working with many stakeholders and customers, building relationships, teaching, working with marketing teams, web teams and PR to synergize efforts, handling tons of communication in a timely manner, creating and delivering reports with metrics tied to organizational goals, and all within a start-up in an existing Firm. It appears to me that I'm now doing the same work, just with a different title, different deliverables, and different clients. I think I've just re-purposed myself.

I now have much more flexibility in my schedule, the location where I work at, who I work with, and on what subjects I spend my time on. And, I still work with my ex-Andersen Partners on occasion (which I really enjoy), travel is minimal, and I don't have to commute downtown everyday. This is great!

I have no idea what the moral of the story is. I do know that if I hadn't networked, I wouldn't be working today. If I hadn't been willing or flexible enough to do part-time contract work while I continued looking for a job, I wouldn't be working today. If I hadn't taken the advice of those people I met at networking events who said don't give up until they say no, I wouldn't be working today. If I hadn't gone to networking meetings, I wouldn't even have had people to give me advice.

So although a lot of people seem to think that just because they go to networking events that the outcome is 'supposed' to be a job, all I have to say to that is there are many skills you develop JUST by the mere act of networking that may never result in an immediate job. However, those skills along with learning how to handle the emotions that go with networking/looking for meaningful work, will certainly change your life, as it's done mine. AND, just because you had one job title before, doesn't mean that that title defines you. It might behoove others to take an inventory of their skills and re-think their next move. I would never have even thought this way about my career, until Crowe approached me about being Editor. After that, I felt like a real idiot. Why hadn't I considered this way of thinking about myself before???

Now I'm wondering if in my future, I'll go live in that cabin in the mountains by the little tranquil lake and write the great American novel…

Take care and thank you for developing and growing Gray Hair Management.

Mary Ann Markowicz

E-Mail 11

I am very pleased to tell you I have started my new position as Associate Vice President, Financial Analysis and Strategy at the Illinois Institute of Technology. My search lasted seven months, consisted of over 200 networking meetings and has resulted in a terrific position.

Members of the network may be interested to note that this position resulted from a fifth level network contact:

1.My friend Randy introduced me to his friend Steve.

2.Steve introduced me to his boss Jim.

3.Jim introduced me to his business contact Joel.

4.Joel introduced me to the CFO of IIT, his former position.

5.John, the CFO of IIT, made me an offer to join his staff two weeks after I networked with him.

Clearly, networking does work. Of particular note, in each of the above cases, I met with the individuals and asked to be introduced to specific contacts that I knew they had. My network became much more robust when I "grew it" by asking for very specific introductions at each level. This led me to contacts who flew in the right circles and who, in turn, could introduce me to specific contacts that I knew they had (or should have through their positions).

I will, of course, be glad to assist other Gray Hair members if I can. Thanks to you for the great networking breakfasts and a terrific website.

Sincerely,
John D. Sinsheimer

GOING FORWARD

As this chapter title indicates, your success in winning the job race can be a function of one or many factors ranging from pure luck to following a comprehensive plan of attack. If you choose to succeed through luck and get lucky, congratulations, and remember that experienced, proven executives can expect to change jobs every 1.8 to three years. Next time you may not be so lucky. We recommend that you commit to succeed by developing the mind set, the skills and the team to maximize your chances of professional job success over a long-term number of years if you:

◆ Need a job.

◆ Want a better job.

◆ Are tired of the extra hours you have been working since your company had a 10% reduction in work force while the amount of work to be done has increased.

◆ Feel like a "rookie" as you look for a job and need professional help finding the right opportunity.

◆ Have had no career growth and no advancement opportunities.

◆ Have reached the ceiling in your current position.

◆ Are underpaid, and your talents and abilities are underutilized and unrecognized.

◆ Are overdue for promotion or been passed over for promotion.

◆ Have been with one company for many years and don't recognize your options.

◆ Are concerned about your age.

◆ Are concerned about the future of your position and uncertain about your career choices in today's business climate.

◆ Work for a company going through organizational change, and you don't know where you stand.

When we first stated working, the Social Security Administration defined the official retirement age (when you could receive full benefits) as 62. If you retire today, it is 65. For us (in the born 1943-1954 years) it is projected to be 66. For anyone born after 1960 it is projected to be 67. The only certainties are the official retirement age will keep increasing, and we will keep living longer. Since more than 80% of the baby boomers working polled (1998 AARP and 1997 Yakoboski and Dickemper research) said they expect to work after "retirement," a large percentage of us will be competing to win the job race again and again. Are you ready?

Developing the job race attitude and techniques outlined in <u>Winning the Job Race: Pathways Through Transition</u> is not easy. On the other hand, it is not as difficult as becoming a rocket scientist or a surgeon either. It starts with a commitment on your part to win the job race again and again and again. It starts with a recognition that companies want to know what you just did for them rather than how loyal and hard working you have been. It starts with a mental frame of mind that approaches each business situation and opportunity with the question, "How can I help you?" It starts with your desire to become the Jimmy

Chitwood (from the movie "Hoosiers") player on your MyPB Company.

It can be done. So we wish you every success in the world as you seek your next job opportunity and improve your career. In conclusion, remember that people successfully change when they personally take ownership for the change. Take ownership! Take control of your career, and make things happen. You can do it. And let us know how you do. We are easy to reach.

Good luck.

jack@grayhairmanagement.com

scott@grayhairmanagement.com

INDEX

Jack Heyden has held senior executive positions in the financial services and consulting industries. Early in his career he was a bank corporate lending officer, operations officer and head of global training and development for a top ten U.S. bank. He then founded his own training and coaching business, and clients included Citicorp, Kraft, FMC, TRW and Nationwide Insurance. For 13 years he was president of a banking association, a position he held until a merger. As GHM's senior coach and mentor, Jack utilizes his extensive experience in executive assessment, coaching, and management and sales development to help clients win the job race.

Scott Kane, GHM founder, has held senior executive positions in the teleproduction and advertising industries for over 30 years. Some of his projects as a Producer-Director were Big 10 Basketball for NBC, NCAA Basketball for HBO and Live Aid. Later in his career he joined Telemation Productions in Chicago as a television producer/director, and worked his way up to Executive Vice President. For six years Scott was President of Optimus, a wholly owned subsidiary of Anheuser-Busch. Scott's extensive experience in marketing, advertising and branding provides GHM clients with the creative strategy they need to help them to differentiate themselves in today's competitive job market.

HELP SOMEONE ELSE
WIN THE JOB RACE

To order individual copies of Winning the Job Race:
Pathways Through Transition":

Go to www.grayhairmanagement.com

To arrange for bulk purchases of the Book:

Telephone 1-847-940-2800

If you would like to have Jack Heyden and/or Scott Kane
speak at your organization's next business meeting,
conference or convention:

E-mail contact@grayhairmanagement.com
or
Telephone 1-847-940-2800

Thank you.

Printed in the United States
26375LVS00006B/259-510

9 780976 610908